I0804873

The Marxian Imagination

The Marxian Imagination

Representing Class in Literature

JULIAN MARKELS

MONTHLY REVIEW PRESS

New York

Library of Congress Cataloging-in-Publication Data

Markels, Julian.
The Marxian imagination : representing class in literature / Julian Markels.
p. cm.
Includes bibliographical references and index.

ISBN 1-58367-098-x (cloth)
ISBN 1-58367-097-1 (pbk)

1. English fiction—History and criticism. 2. Social classes in literature. 3. American fiction—History and criticism. 4. Marxist criticism. I. Title.
PR830.S6M37 2003
823.009'355—dc21

MONTHLY REVIEW PRESS
122 West 27th Street
New York, NY 10001

www.monthlyreview.org

Printed in Canada

10 9 8 7 6 5 4 3 2 1

For Willie, with love and thanks

The most interesting and difficult part of any cultural analysis, in complex societies, is that which seeks to grasp the hegemonic in its active and formative, but also its transformational processes. Works of art, by their substantial and general character, are often especially important as sources for this complex evidence.

— RAYMOND WILLIAMS

Class is an adjective, not a noun.

— STEPHEN A. RESNICK and RICHARD D. WOLFF

ACKNOWLEDGMENTS

My references throughout this book to Stephen A. Resnick and Richard D. Wolff's *Knowledge and Class* only begin to indicate my debt to their work. Resnick and Wolff enabled me conceptually to undertake my project, and that project has given me a deeply satisfying scholarly retirement. Second only to them in inspiring my effort has been Ellen Meiksins Wood in the whole range of her writing. To have read at the feet of these Marxist scholars has been the belated privilege of a now long lifetime, and I can only hope my book might prove worthy of their influence on it.

Robin Bell Markels is my necessary reader and rhetorical mentor: her canons of scholarship and practical intelligence have everywhere guided my effort and sustained me in my purpose. James Kincaid is in his third decade of reading my manuscripts, and he keeps doing it with an incisive thoroughness and loving care for which I can never thank him enough. J. Ronald Green read this manuscript with the compositional insight of an exceptional film critic, and his criticisms have been absolutely indispensable. Walter A. Davis, Marlene Longenecker, Ken Petri, Eric Schocket, and Susan Yadlon made crucial suggestions for improving individual chapters; James Phelan gave me just the right advice at just the right time for my form of presentation; and Jason Payne put me on to important materials just when I needed them. I have also depended throughout on the support of Michael Andes, Steven Fink, Mimi Harris, Audrey Jaffe, and Elizabeth Renker.

My three children are spending their lives in the helping professions, and while they don't share my Marxism, our conversation keeps reminding me how my abstract Marxian interests are rooted in the concrete daily damage done by class expropriation to millions of people who must depend one-by-one on the helping professions. Every day in my heart I thank Alex, Linda, and Rachel for their quiet courage and hands-on wisdom.

Three of my chapters have been previously published in an earlier form and appear here with permission: "Toward a Marxian Reentry to the Novel," *Narrative* 4.3 (1996), 197–217; "The Representation of Class in the Realist Novel," *Rethinking Marxism* 11.3 (1999), 20–35; and "'Socialism-Anxiety': *The Princess Casamassima* and Its New York Critics," *College Literature* 27.2 (2000), 37–56.

PART ONE

The Literary Representation of Class

1

A MARXIAN IMAGINATION

My title echoes that of Lionel Trilling's *The Liberal Imagination*, and my book parallels his in seeking to identify a literary imagination that abstracts a political master narrative which engages us intellectually and moves us emotionally in and through its poetic, dramaturgic, or novelistic representation. Whatever Trilling's differences with Marxism, his conception of this imagination is germane to my purpose in two key respects. First, he claims that "between sentiments and ideas there is a natural connection so close as to amount to a kind of identity"—which can also mean an identity between literature and politics:

> What comes in to being when two contradictory emotions are made to confront each other and are required to have a relationship with each other is . . . quite properly called an idea. Ideas may also be said to be generated in the opposition of ideals, and in the felt awareness of the impact of new circumstances upon old forms of feeling and estimation, in the response to the conflict between new exigencies and old pieties.[1]

Here imagination involves an interpenetration of thought and feeling in which the personal becomes political not in abstract reflection after the fact but in the contradictions and stress of lived experience. The literary representation of this experience is then necessarily informed by ideas, whether explicit or implicit, and our response to it is shaped in part by the cognitive configuration of those ideas.

Second, Trilling claims that any given politics has its own imagination, which seeks to represent the personal as political specifically in respect to that politics. Thus he warns that liberalism, which he calls America's sole intellectual tradition, must be especially self-critical,

> for in the very interest of its great primal act of imagination by which it establishes its essence and existence—in the interest, that is, of its vision of a general enlargement and freedom and rational direction of human life—it drifts towards a denial of the emotions and the imagination. (xiii)

And he says that the job of literary criticism is "to recall liberalism to its first essential imagination of variousness and possibility, which implies the awareness of complexity and difficulty" (xv). These references to a primal act of imagination, and then a first essential imagination, attribute to liberalism a foundational, master narrative of enlargement and freedom achieved through engagement with complexity and difficulty—or what contemporary cultural theory would call a humanist pluralism. Then Trilling's essays in *The Liberal Imagination* single out topics and texts through whose analysis he can reaffirm liberalism's master narrative of socially indeterminate pluralism.

From a political standpoint opposed to Trilling's, I argue correspondingly that Marxism establishes its existence, as an intellectual tradition certainly as powerful as liberalism, by a primal act of imagination. This is its imagination of the enlargement of life and freedom specifically promised by the abolition of class, when class is understood as an overdetermined process of appropriating and distributing surplus labor without consulting those who perform the labor. This historically structured process precludes any immediate or universal enlargement of freedom in which variousness and possibility, complexity and difficulty, might become ends in themselves. Marx may have dreamed of a far-off day when we could all work in the morning, write poetry in the afternoon, and go fishing after dinner (or vice versa), in a life wonderfully conducive to possibility, complexity, and what Trilling's mentor Matthew Arnold called "the free play of the mind upon all subjects." But for now Marx accepted the need to focus his mind—and thus his "ism"—on the social construction of class processes and relations, fraught through and through with a complexity of their own, by which any play of mind is ideologically circumscribed at any given moment of our historical finitude.

From within this Marxian focus, the job I have then attempted is narrow and even primitive: first, to identify individually a representative sampling of literary works that struggle toward Marxism's first essential imagination of class; and second, to suggest some implications of this struggle for understanding the relation of literature to culture and society.[2] My procedure, like Trilling's, has been to stalk the literary terrain for particular examples, and I think the range of difference among the texts I have chosen—in historical, biographical, or ideological circumstances, in gender, ethnic, or class markings, in rhetorical coherence and power—is sufficient to constitute a concrete phenomenon. Just as Marx himself struggled to enter the imagination of class specifically as a process of expropriation, so too on occasion did Shakespeare and Alexander Saxton, Dickens and Barbara Kingsolver, Henry James and Meridel Le Sueur, among others I discuss.

Several of my writers were specifically influenced by Marx, whether directly or indirectly, while others anticipated him or else arrived independently at his central insight. But that they all shared in his imaginative struggle is illustrated by, among other things, the plot deformations of individual works, for example, *King Lear*, *Hard Times*, *The Girl*, and *The Great Midland*; by the relations between works in a single writer's canon, for example, *Hard Times* and *Little Dorrit*, *The Girl* and *I Hear Men Talking*, *Animal Dreams* and *The Poisonwood Bible*; and by the relations between writers' lives and works, for example, James's letters and *The Princess Casamassima*, Le Sueur's socialist heritage and all her fiction, or Dickens's and Kingsolver's engagement with their audience. This various and complex struggle in their medium enlarges the cognitive significance of Marx's struggle in his, and it is not simply personal but a social and historical struggle whose significance contemporary cultural theory has no way to recognize.

It is also a struggle regularly marked by tragedy—the tragic careers of writers like Le Sueur who keep striving toward a Marxian imagination and the tragic forms of writers like Shakespeare and James who reluctantly reach it. Such multiform tragedy is what Marxism conceivably could lead us to expect: a resistance to its imagination, ingrained in the texture of bourgeois culture and consciousness, which then makes its impact and value all the greater for being so rare. But that value can be realized only by a Marxism that provides theoretically for the imagination I try to identify, and I also try to show how the two most influential Marxian cultural theorists recently writing in English, Raymond Williams and Fredric Jameson, both fail to provide for this imagination. Different as they are in other respects, both treat the literary text as politically unconscious and thus as a fragmenting object of our theory rather than a constitutive agent itself, capable of making its own breakthroughs to a knowledge and feeling we don't yet have and can't find elsewhere. In so doing, Williams and Jameson both absorb literature into a Marxian sociology which is thereby enriched, but which also erases the knowledge, pleasure, and power intrinsic to literary representation.

Insofar as my project then reflects what F. S. C. Northrop once called the "natural history" stage of inquiry[3]—the stage at which one collects samples of a phenomenon that looks significant but whose significance is not recognized by current theory whether Marxian or non-Marxian—I suppose I am making what is called a theoretical "intervention." But it is also substantially a theoretical reversion, in its effort to stand back from current theory so as to rethink a Marxian humanism comparable to Trilling's liberal humanism with its conception of a literary imagination that is rejected by current theory. Thus while I address theoretical issues specifically relevant to my writers in their struggle—class as process versus class as identity; symbolic coherence versus narrative coherence; Lukacs's realism, Gramsci's organicism, and Williams's structures of feeling—my purpose most often is to challenge contemporary theory on behalf of this Marxian humanism. Only in the chapter on Williams and Jameson do I attempt a comprehensive theoretical critique, and there I am trying to insert where it belongs—within a rethought Marxism—the "natural history" that I believe my inquiry has uncovered.

1

The concept of class as a social process both historically structured and continuously overdetermined is not widely shared among contemporary cultural scholars. Characteristically for them, class is a homogeneous identity site, like gender, ethnicity, or sexual orientation, where people are subject to domination or oppression. African-American women factory workers at their site, for example, are said to experience differences of vocational or educational opportunity, of health care or child care, of income or self-concept, that produce different feminist agendas from those of white homemakers at their site or lesbian professionals at theirs. When contemporary cultural scholars do concern themselves with class, they treat it most often as a geographical difference of this kind.

Yet coextensive with such differences is a single experience common to the great majority of women at all three identity sites mentioned above—that they perform surplus labor and that the product of this labor, whether in the form of canned soup or the family laundry or "billable hours," is appropriated and distributed without their having any say in how that is done. This experience remains invisible to current scholarship as well as to its participants for a variety of reasons. First is institutional resistance to (or evasion of) the discourse of class specifically as expropriation. With rare exceptions nowadays, this Marxian discourse decertifies an academic in the social sciences, while certified Marxists in the humanities are those for whose Marxism expropriation is passé—as it is for Fredric Jameson when he says that "*Ressentiment* is the primal class passion" and then expatiates on class as an identity site of envy and hatred to which the fact of expropriation is evidently irrelevant.[4]

Second, gender, ethnicity, and sexual orientation, and very often occupation and income as well, are written on the body—in physiology, physiognomy, and pigmentation, in dress, ornament, and ideolect, in body language itself—as material identities through which people become subject to domination and oppression. But capitalism's relations of production in which these people are compelled to participate, although themselves material relations, are not thus directly visible. They are a dirty secret to be theoretically inferred, and, beginning with Marx's deconstruction of "appearances" like commodities and money, inferring them requires a leap of imagination that is not ordinarily required to recognize gender, ethnicity, or queerness as sites of domination and oppression.

Third, class may resist recognition because as a collective identity and geographical location, it remains for us all something ultimately to be abolished rather than celebrated and preserved. "Class is an adjective, not a noun," insist Resnick and Wolff in *Knowledge and Class*,[5] and the point of class struggle, an expression which they say "must refer to the object of groups struggling, not to the subjects doing the struggling" (*KC*, 161), is to dissolve these groups by putting an end to expropriation. Class is not just materially less visible but theoretically more transient than is easy to imagine for gender, ethnicity, or sexual orientation: proletarians need to be celebrated only for as long as expropriation continues, whereas women, ethnics, and queers are always and everywhere to be celebrated not abolished.[6]

In fact, gender, ethnicity, and sexual orientation also have been theorized as social processes rather than identity sites,[7] but their material embodiments exert a kind of downward pull on their theoretical status. The immediate otherness of physiognomy or behavior cries out to be humanly accepted even before it gets theorized and no matter how it gets theorized, whereas the otherness of class is initially more abstract and experientially mediated.

Finally, class may be subject to lip service only in contemporary scholarship simply because it is Marxism's master narrative, and to treat it as other than an identity site is to risk being implicated *a priori* in a notoriously oversimplified version of the Marxian narrative—that class is determined by an objective relationship to the mode of production and that, being so determined, class as base determines the superstructural and subjective oppressions of gender, ethnicity, and queerness. But that is not the version of Marxism on which I rely in this book, and while here is not the place to rehearse in detail the Marxian literature on class, let me at least outline a more complex class theory, derived principally from the work of E. P. Thompson and of Resnick and Wolff, that informs my project.

These scholars begin by defining class as a process of social reproduction wherein, in Marx's familiar formulation, "unpaid surplus labor is pumped out of the direct producers." Resnick and Wolff then distinguish between this direct expropriation, which they call the "fundamental class process," and the "subsumed class processes" (*KC,* 118) through which the appropriated surplus is distributed and received. These subsumed processes are embodied in the social infrastructure—financial and political, educational and cultural—necessary to facilitate and protect the fundamental class process as conditions of its existence.

All these processes are objective and determinate. Whether as slave, feudal, or capitalist fundamental processes of expropriation, or as banking, legislative, or cultural subsumed processes of distribution and reception, they occur specifically as class processes independently of any subjective recognition of their class character. The class process is objectively present to be experienced, but there is nothing necessary or inevitable in people's experiencing it in what Thompson called "class ways."[8]

Thompson's account of class is especially relevant to literary representation because it insists on the particularity of lived experience: he conducts a running critique of statistical and generalizing theories of class, and of Marxian metaphors of base and superstructure that "congeal a fluent social process" ("Eighteenth-Century," 152), while also amassing mountainous evidence that exhibits historical subjects behaving like characters in a play or novel in responding to their experience in "class ways." Even so, Thompson's great studies of class, in *The Making of the English Working Class* and *Customs in Common*, leave off without reaching just those particulars of historical experience whose contradictions and overdeterminations constitute a subject matter for the literary imagination. Sensitive as he is to the "inefficient ways" and "cultural lags"[9] through which class formation occurs, Thompson has no way to focus on inefficiency and lag as themselves materially necessary to the formative process—that is, on the complex present of frequently tragic personal life that motivated his attempt to "rescue the poor stockinger . . . the 'obsolete' handloom weaver, the utopian artisan . . . from the enormous condescension of posterity" (*MEWC*, 12).

Thompson begins *The Making of the English Working Class* by claiming that

> . . . class happens when some men, as a result of common experiences . . . feel and articulate the identity of their interests as between themselves, and as against other men whose interests are different from (and usually opposed to) theirs. The class experience is largely determined by the productive relations into which men are born . . . Class consciousness is the way in which these experiences are handled in cultural terms . . . . If the experience appears as determined, class-consciousness does not. We can see a *logic* in the response of similar occupational groups undergoing similar experiences, but we cannot predicate any *law*. (*MEWC*, 9–10; emphasis in text)

Fifteen years later, during which he did much of the work for *Customs in Common*, Thompson explicitly reaffirms this conception and elaborates as follows:

> We know about class because people have repeatedly behaved in class ways: these historical events disclose regularities of response to analogous situations, and at a certain stage (the "mature" formations of class) we observe the creation of institutions, and of a culture with class notations, which admits of transnational comparisons. ("Eighteenth Century," 147)

But while there may be only a logic and not a law by which people come to recognize their identity of interests in opposition to others', that logic becomes apparent only after the fact and may exclude along the way any number of people who do not recognize as fully as others (and perhaps not at all) either their identity or opposition of interests. Non-class behavior is as much a "regularity of response" as class behavior, and Thompson himself speaks of potential class members who for most of a century "were consenting adults in their own corruption" ("Eighteenth-Century," 142). That I think is why he needs his own generalizing terms—"class *ways*," "class *notations*," and "*mature* class formations"—to accommodate the erratic, inefficient, and more often than not evanescent, formation of a working class with its consciousness. For all his historian's particularity, his historian's method gives him limited access to the individual lives through whose conflicts and stress some but not all of his stockingers, weavers, and artisans came to recognize their identity or opposition of interests. A fuller access to those personal lives is precisely the aim of literary representation.

Some weavers did and some did not experience class processes in "class ways" because, as Resnick and Wolff tirelessly insist, their experience was and is always overdetermined by multiple, overlapping, often contradictory, social conditions and processes:

> Human beings may participate in fundamental or subsumed class processes or both or neither. However, to the degree that they do participate in one or both, they occupy positions within them: performers or appropriators of surplus labor and/or distributors or recipients of shares of appropriated surplus labor. They occupy class positions that are overdetermined and hence contradictory. Each person also occupies a specific subset of other, *nonclass* positions within comparably overdetermined and contradictory nonclass social processes . . .
>
> How human beings resolve the overdetermined contradictions within which they pass their lives depends on the interactions between and among the social processes in which they occupy positions and those in which they do not. Human beings are shaped both by the class positions they hold and those they do not hold. . . . The same is true of all the nonclass positions within society. (*KC*, 159–60; emphasis in text)

People who perform surplus labor may also be people who receive distributions of appropriated surplus or otherwise occupy what another theorist, Erik Olin Wright, calls "contradictory class locations."[10] People's response to participating in class processes may also conflict with, and be overdetermined by, their response to participating in any number of non-class processes like summer-league softball or singing *The Messiah* at Christmas. Amidst the welter of overdetermination through which any person transacts an individual life, the collective identity indicated by such terms as class ways, (mature) class consciousness, and class culture can become sufficiently problematic to resist representation by anything less than a literary leap of faith and imagination.

2

It was Althusser who introduced into Marxian theory the concept of overdetermination, and I share his avowed discomfort in doing so:

> I am not particularly taken by this term *overdetermination* (borrowed from other disciplines), but I shall use it in the absence of anything better, both as an *index* and as a *problem* ...[11]

It is an ugly, distracting, easily misunderstood term, but as index and problem it is uniquely capable of challenging the misapprehensions and evasions common to so much class analysis, Marxian and non-Marxian, which fails to see how intricately expropriation is embedded in historical life and is thus so resistant to recognition and representation.

As index, the concept of overdetermination can identify the twin failures of base-superstructure Marxism and identity-site classism in their one-dimensional conceptions of social determination. As problem, the concept of overdetermination can itself collapse into an ahistorical concept of random contingency subject only to discourse, which it often seems to do in the later attempts of Resnick and Wolff and their Althusserian colleagues to articulate what they call a "postmodern materialism." On the one hand, their breakthrough in explaining expropriation as an overdetermined process facilitates a rethought Marxism that can account for the particularities of everyday life which other class theories (including Thompson's) ignore but which all of us know as personal experience:

> An individual is the site, for example, of the effects of class, parents, jobs, religions, politics, literature, biology, and so on. So too is an enterprise, a literary text, or a political party. At such sites, each entity comprises or contains different effects that push and pull it in all directions with varying force.

On the other hand, their analysis of class as one among many stories to be told of an individual, an enterprise, a text, or a party, leaves it unclear how the varying forces pushing and pulling in all directions could ever have produced historically anything like Marxism's specified progression of class structures and relations from slave to feudal to capitalist to communist:

> Moreover, in a world of ideas and actions now cast adrift from any guaranteeing anchors or determining foundations, all theories and political movements become merely different from one another, alternative stories or accounts of social life.[12]

They note that Althusser himself struggled with the concept of overdetermination, and they reject his qualifying corollary of "determination in the last instance" as a fatal reversion to base-superstructure Marxism. But in throwing out the modernist bathwater of base and superstructure so as to provide for nothing more than postmodern pushing and shoving in all directions by telling stories, Resnick and Wolff often seem ready to abandon Marxism's constitutive logic of historical change—the logic but not the law of Thompson's structured processes evoking "regularities of response."

In this respect Resnick and Wolff and their colleagues may still be open to the critique of Althusserianism made by Ellen Meiksins Wood in *The Retreat from Class*, published the same year as *Knowledge and Class*. For the Althusserians she was criticizing, Wood argued,

> The "mode of production" as a structure of determined relations does not exist empirically. In the "social formation" that *does* exist empirically, structural *relations* are replaced by "conjunctures" and juxtapositions, an arbitrary configuration of "over-determined" elements (the potentially useful concept of over-determination has increasingly become a cover for absolute contingency). In the historical world of the social formation, there are no relations to be explained, only juxtapositions to be described—even if description can be given an air of theoretical "rigor" and determinacy by means of classification in an endless proliferation of taxonomic categories. The structural relations of the mode of production have no explanatory status, since they do not reflect the logic of any actually existing historical and social processes.[13]

Yet for my purpose in this book, the problem of overdetermination as contingency need not limit its function as an index to literary representation. What Wood calls the potential usefulness of the concept is its insistence on the complex push-and-pull of multiple forces as the real-life medium in which we in fact participate in structured relations like class. The literary representation of this real-life interplay—of the human comedy, tragedy, spectacle—has always proved engaging in itself, and has also proved necessary to make persuasive any thematized representation of relations like class that might be embedded within it. When George Eliot's narrator says in *Middlemarch*,

> I at least have so much to do in unraveling certain human lots, and seeing how they were woven and interwoven, that all the light I can command must be thrown on this particular web, and not dispersed over that tempting range of relevancies called the universe,[14]

she is explaining why she doesn't have the rhetorical leisure for Fielding's philosophical digressions. But she is also claiming in effect that representing overdetermination—the raveled web of human lots—is both a project sufficient unto itself, as it clearly is in *Middlemarch*, and also a prerequisite for representing such relevancies as Fielding's philosophical topics or a Marxist's class processes. The imaginative struggle of the writers I discuss is in fact to do both, to see (or not see), through the rhetorical process of producing narratives of overdetermination, the social processes in which expropriation is mediated as personal experience.

3

The effort to understand this imaginative struggle is greatly facilitated by another key concept of Resnick and Wolff's, "point of entry." However debatable their global deployment of the concept of overdetermination, where literary narrative is concerned "point of entry" makes that concept functional by providing the necessary link between Marxism's master narrative of structured class processes and a narrative like Eliot's of interwoven human lots. Resnick and Wolff argue that the dense web of overdetermination among social processes can never be comprehensively analyzed and that Marxism, like all other theories, must choose for its analysis a point of entry which is necessarily incomplete and thus necessarily partisan—the concept of class as expropriation. Other theories like Freudianism or Social Darwinism require other points of entry for their master narratives, and Resnick and Wolff argue for a historically *particularized* relativism of theories—a relativism which recognizes that all theories are ideologically situated and politically partisan, so that a pluralist conversation among them cannot itself be universalized but instead must be historicized as a form of contestation. Thus Marxian theory, like any other theory, "has, as one of its conditions of existence, the intentions of its practitioners to accomplish the predominance of Marxian over other theories. Such predominance is a condition of existence for other social changes sought by Marxists" (*KC*, 36–7). Yet if Marxian theory should achieve predominance, and along with it the social changes for which it is a condition of existence, it could not then make an essentialist claim to have arrived at a "truth" that mirrors "reality." For Resnick and Wolff it would still be open in principle to successful challenge by other theories, some of whose conditions for existence might have meanwhile emerged just as Marxism's did at a particular time.[15]

Or in other words, Marxism's or Freudianism's or Social Darwinism's master narrative—of expropriation, or libido and superego, or survival of the fittest—can be made the organizing principle of a literary narrative just as it can of a social theory. The representation of overdetermined social processes in epic, romance, drama, or novel is necessarily more selective than the data sorted and assembled by social theory, and asks to be apprehended immediately in the experience of reading. When a work is in fact governed by a "master narrative," which is certainly not always the case, a full apprehension of that work will include its point of entry, with its particular configuration of overdetermined social processes, as an autonomous epistemological project. That is, a reader immersed in the work's narratological dynamics from the beginning takes pleasure along the way in recognizing as it unfolds this work's principle of form, along with its emerging criteria for closure (or non-closure), whether or not those criteria are being met. This response to the work's holistic progression makes us aware of its point of entry—and also, in some very telling cases, of its author's rhetorical and epistemological struggle to establish or avoid that point of entry with the master narrative it entails.

4

On the understanding of class as a historically structured, socially invisible, overdetermined process of transient expropriation, I argue that the representation of class requires the abstracting power of imagination—the power to find what Henry James would call the figure of class in the carpet of overdetermination—that Lionel Trilling ascribes to the political master narrative. This power is typically manifested neither in direct representation of performed surplus labor nor in "thick description" of proletarian poverty and struggle. For to write about class is not necessarily to write about people belonging to a single class at its identity site. It is rather to write what becomes intelligible and coherent only through its understanding of class as a process of expropriation. Not being directly visible, this process can only be represented indirectly, and its indirect manifestations need to be represented with sufficient variety and scope to produce a literary structure through whose point of entry class is overtly thematized and not left to be retrieved from a political unconscious.[16]

Thus conceived, the imagination of class entails a Marxian humanism very different from that of "the proletarian sublime" in its capacity to produce a wide variety of literary structures and aesthetic effects—from that of a metaphorical domestic novel like *Little Dorrit* to that of a realist strike novel like *To Make My Bread* to that of a tragic *Bildungsroman* like *The Princess Casamassima* to that of a historical novel like *The Poisonwood Bible*. Both historically and rhetorically, the realist novel has been the genre most accommodating to the imagination of class, and in Chapter Three I try to explain why that genre is especially well suited, although certainly not obligated, to represent class as a hidden process of expropriation rather than a visible identity site. But mine is not an attempt to vindicate Marxian theories of realism that make it an exclusive medium for representing class. I pay special attention to the realist novel because I think that for cultural scholars as for lay readers (who remain devoted to it by the millions), its imagination of class as process can serve as a benchmark for metaphorical and symbolic forms that are conspicuously vulnerable to eliding class into an identity site.[17] But as I hope will become evident, it is also crucial to my project to see a Marxian imagination at work in non-realist works such as those I discuss by Shakespeare, Dickens, and Kingsolver.

The variety of genres in which class appears as process also resists the distinction between canonical and non-canonical literary works customarily made on geographical grounds of identity affirmation. The white male heterosexual literary canon is customarily said not simply to suppress the voices of women and others, but also to establish modes of cognition and terms of discourse that keep these Others forever mute. Yet the imagination of class as expropriation, with the particular cognition that entails, links canonical writers like Shakespeare, Dickens, and James with insurgent writers like Lumpkin, Le Sueur, and Alexander Saxton who represent class as the presiding yet overdetermined process shaping their characters' lives, while also excluding insurgent writers like Harriette Arnow, Toni Morrison, and Tillie Olsen who represent class as their characters' identity site of material deprivation and ideological stress.[18] Class as master narrative, then, in producing its alternative canon to that of liberal white male heterosexuality, also tears asunder the ostensibly homogeneous multicultural "anti-canon" produced by liberalism's loyal opposition—feminist, ethnic, or queer—to white male heterosexuality.

5

Let me try to illustrate all this provisionally here by juxtaposing Arnow's *The Dollmaker*, a realist novel fundamentally innocent of the imagination of class, with no less than *King Lear*, a metaphorical drama fundamentally constituted by that imagination. Like *King Lear*, *The Dollmaker* is often said to be an unforgettably moving personal experience.[19] My dear mother, who grew up reading Balzac, Dickens, and Shakespeare at the Carnegie Library in Goshen, Indiana, could never find enough right words for *The Dollmaker*, and neither can Joyce Carol Oates in her afterword to its latest reprint. Oates says that "this brutal, beautiful novel has a permanent effect upon the reader"; then, that "one is convinced, partway through the book, that it is a masterpiece" no matter how it might turn out; and, finally, that

> There are certainly greater novels than *The Dollmaker*, but I can think of none that have moved me more, personally, terrifyingly, involving me in the solid fact of life's criminal exploitation of those who live it—not hard, not sentimental, not at all intellectually ambitious, *The Dollmaker* is one of those excellent American works that have yet to be properly assessed.[20]

Oates's poignant ambiguity speaks for me, my mother, and I imagine most others: even partway through one wants to call this a masterpiece, yet one also knows there are greater novels. I think this ambiguity (properly assessed!) arises from the way *The Dollmaker* actively produces intellectual ambitions which it then declines to pursue. Arnow's comprehensiveness and complexity in depicting hillbilly steelworkers' heart-rending experience at their social location also excludes any meaningful response to this experience, by the characters, their narrator, or their author, in "class ways." While this exclusion may actually contribute to *The Dollmaker*'s rhetorical power, it also circumscribes the novel as a pastoral ethnography that lacks the aesthetic and cognitive resonance of some greater novels.

The Dollmaker depicts the 1944 migration from a Kentucky hill farm to a Detroit housing project of Gertie Nevels, her husband Clovis, and their five children. Clovis gets a wartime job in the steel mill, Gertie and the children join him after 150 pages, and the remaining 450 pages depict the first year of the family's struggle to survive urban poverty. In this bare outline their story lends itself perfectly to a classic Marxian narrative of farmers losing access to the land and being forced to sell their labor to urban capitalists who then pump out of their production as much unpaid surplus as will allow these workers only a bare subsistence.

Such a narrative was clearly implied, through a variety of rhetorical methods (some better than others), in the half-dozen 1930s novels depicting the 1929 Gastonia, North Carolina, strike of similarly proletarianized hill farmers. But in contrast to those novels, four of which I will discuss in Chapter Three, *The Dollmaker*'s resolute pastoralism produces urbanization rather than class as point of entry and organizing principle, and thus conspicuously avoids this Marxian narrative. Its insistent focus is on the contrast between rural and urban life—fresh and foul air and food, artisan crafts and mass-produced commodities, houses set amidst gardens and fields and party-wall apartments amidst debris-filled yards—and then on the need to "adjust," a word repeated throughout the novel, from the one to the other. Clovis being a mechanic by temperament and vocation, the ordeal of adjustment falls to Gertie and the children, of whom three survive it and two don't. Reuben, the eldest, runs away at age 12 back to Kentucky, and Cassie, the fourth child and a literary creation worthy of Dickens or Tolstoy, is killed by a train while conversing with her imaginary companion, a wooden doll carved by her mother. Gertie's involvement in Cassie's death, and her temporary madness following it, are as stunningly rendered as the suicide of Kirilov or the madness of Lear, and I think it is principally this extended episode that makes *The Dollmaker* so deeply moving.

Also moving in a more compromised fashion is the novel's central saga of Gertie's ordeal of adjustment. In its opening Kentucky episode she is a female Paul Bunyan, persuading strangers by sheer determination to drive her sick child to a hospital while she performs a backseat tracheotomy that allows this child to breathe until they arrive. But then Arnow's ethnographic purpose and pastoral point of entry reduce Gertie permanently to impotence once she arrives in Detroit. Larger than life as she's been at everything connected with rural existence, in the city she is cowed, bewildered, and constantly guilt-ridden for being so. She has no fingertip instincts for dealing with produce vendors, schoolteachers, or even her husband and children in their response to a strange new environment, and she is never allowed to acquire any. Instead, she remains a *tabula* on which the city inscribes its horrors.

Arnow's depiction of these horrors is not only massive but textured and complex. In a small-print, 17-page chapter devoted to Gertie's walking her children to their first day of school in Detroit, we get descriptions not only of the filthy snow, slushy sidewalks, and dangerous streets (among other things) but also (among other things) of the cultural crosscurrents among the Catholic and Protestant children walking with them, some of whom mock the new "hillbillies" while others befriend them, and then of the dingy school, crowded classrooms, and stressed-out teachers who nevertheless greet them in quite different ways, some friendly and caring and some bureaucratically remote.

Through her immersion in this textured world, Gertie becomes both an urban earth mother to her housing project neighbors and a rural Christ figure for the reader. She carves her neighbors crucifixes and dolls, she becomes their confidant, she babysits their children and takes in their laundry. But in all of this she is also their representative sufferer. Disarmed from taking with neighbors, teachers, and even Clovis the initiatives necessary to protect Reuben and Cassie, Gertie feels cripplingly guilty for what happens to both children. And she ought to, for in neither case has she shown even a spark of the mythic strength that saved her youngest at the novel's outset.

In a more symbolic novel this polarized contrast between Gertie the rural maestro and Gertie the urban martyr might feel exactly right; but in a realist novel of massively graduated detail, it feels artificial and strained. Nor is *The Dollmaker*'s sense of strain confined to its treatment of Gertie. It is also evident, for example, in Arnow's rendition of Detroit, whose frigid winter and boiling summer follow each other with only eye-blink intervals for spring and fall, and most of all in her incoherent rendition of the Nevels' response to unionization.

All the housing project steelworkers are regularly short of money for food and clothes, payments on furniture and cars, and even popsicles for their kids in the summer heat. So there is predictably talk of unionization and a strike, which Gertie resists throughout. Early on, we are told that "Gertie had never known there were so many ways for a workingman to die: burned, crushed, skinned alive, smothered, gassed, electrocuted, chopped to bits, blown to pieces,"[21] and yet (on the next page!) that

> Gertie wished Clovis would speak. He hated the unions as much as she . . . A man oughtn't to have to join anything except of his own free will. Free will, free will: only your own place on your own land brought free will. (319)

Later, she wonders why Clovis isn't more pleased when a union steward advocating a strike is beaten up: "it was bad for anybody to get hurt, but if it had to be somebody she was glad it was the man who wanted a strike" (457). And when the strike comes, Gertie prefers to think it is caused by union officials trying simply to consolidate their power. Clovis reminds her that not all the strike advocates are union officials, but then without an ounce of motive gets himself beaten while protecting from company thugs none other than a union official. When he and his friends now defy union discipline and kill the person who beat him, Gertie figures out what they've done, feels ashamed but suffers in silence, and blames everything on the union.

Arnow's focus throughout on the workers' conditions of existence leads her to make unionization an issue. But then she declines to make it also an issue whether the workers' conditions of existence might also be conditions of expropriation. The inchoate mimetic shorthand of the unionization episode, after the painstaking coherence of all that precedes it, denies the characters even the opportunity to react to their experience in "class ways." Its function is rather to reinforce *The Dollmaker*'s presiding pastoralism: unions are one more urban evil, like store-bought food and mass-produced toys, before which Gertie's antipathy remains impotent.

Her only source of potency has been her woodcarving, and this finally enables her to "adjust" to the city as her two children were unable to do. The novel reaches closure on Gertie's insistence that she will hand-carve her dolls for sale rather than mass-produce them on the jigsaw Clovis rigged up for her, and then on her splitting for this purpose the great block of cherrywood she brought from Kentucky. She had been carving in this block a figure that sometimes felt to her like Christ and sometimes, as a projection of herself in betraying her two children, like Judas. But in the novel's final scene, when asked whether she intended Christ, "butcha couldn't find no face fu him," Gertie says, No, there are millions of faces she could have used: "Why, some a my neighbors down there in the alley—they would have done" (599)—and that is *The Dollmaker*'s final sentence.

Those neighbors in Gertie's alley are being martyred by the city and not by anything Arnow's readers can connect meaningfully with class. To be sure, in addition to its unionization episode the novel has made satirical swipes at the factory owner and his minions who live in upscale Grosse Point, just as it has contrasted Gertie's hand-carved dolls with mass-produced toys. But for Arnow's ideological and generic purposes these class and non-class evils are simply lumped together. As Kathleen Parker puts it, "Arnow's antipathy to capitalism remains evident in her portrayal of its effects on the family,"[22] and these effects are represented not as historical effects of expropriation but as geographical effects of urbanization.

Arnow's pastoralism led her to suppress what she may well have recognized as the class implications of her domestic story. Shakespeare in *King Lear*, by contrast, found in his source a domestic story innocent of class and then, as if taking himself by surprise, gave this story class implications whose force impelled him to risk some daring departures from his earlier practice on the way to producing class as *King Lear*'s point of entry.

At the time *King Lear* was written, Shakespeare was not simply what we would call a political conservative; he had no way to conceive class as an abstract category. Yet in what is often considered his most profound and moving tragedy, he imagined a class conflict of Trilling's sentiments-become-ideas, the sentiments of feudalism represented by Cordelia and the sentiments of capitalism represented by Edmund. When Cordelia refuses to exchange a flattering speech for a kingdom and tells her father that

> You have begot me, bred me, lov'd me: I
> Return those duties back as are right fit,
> Obey you, love you, and most honour you (I.i.96–8),

she is also speaking for Kent, Edgar, and Cornwall's servant by expressing in idealized form the ethics specific to a feudal class process wherein surplus labor is appropriated not economically but politically, and the mutual loyalty (and love) of expropriator and expropriated are legitimated by law and custom as protection by the one in return for tribute by the other.[23]

When Edmund dismisses this mutual loyalty (and love) as merely "the plague of custom" and invokes instead "the lusty stealth of nature" to justify his scheming for the kingdom Cordelia has refused, he is also speaking for Goneril, Regan, and Cornwall by expressing in idealized form the ethics specific to a capitalist class process wherein surplus labor is appropriated not politically but economically, in a free market no longer subject to political legitimation but only to "invention":

> Well then,
> Legitimate Edgar, I must have your land,
> Our father's love is to the bastard Edmund
> As to th' legitimate. Fine word, "legitimate"!
> Well, my legitimate, if this letter speed,
> And my invention thrive, Edmund the base
> Shall top th' legitimate—: I grow, I prosper. (I.ii.15–21)

Amidst its mutually overdetermining themes and images—kingship, gender, "Nature"—*King Lear* is comprehensively constituted by its cognition of the conflict between residual feudalism and emergent capitalism as reflected in these speeches of Cordelia and Edmund. It is not, of course, as if Shakespeare recognizes directly the material processes of feudal and capitalist expropriation as I have described them here. It is rather as if he infers them indirectly by polarizing the sentiments of Cordelia and Edmund, who are both responding to their experience in unmistakably "class ways," and who are never both on stage at the same time because their responses are mutually impermeable. Wherever he may have gleaned the sentiments he systematizes in the speeches of Cordelia and Edmund, Shakespeare systematizes their opposition only by an act of imagination whose way of understanding anticipates Marx's understanding of history.

Nor did this cognition come easily to Shakespeare, who is pushed by his own momentum to some daring formal departures. A unique feature of *King Lear*, unprecedented in Shakespeare's practice, is a plot progression that denies the sympathetic (feudal) characters any leverage on the unfolding action and thereby denies the audience any ground for hope that these characters with their sentiments can survive. In writing his tragedies Shakespeare had long since mastered the Aristotelian method of creating suspense by a sequence of episodes that alternately arouse the audience's fears and hopes for the sympathetic characters, so that until the "reversal" we were encouraged to hope that a tragic outcome could be averted. But there is no "reversal" in *King Lear*, where the few episodes that arouse but the barest of hope are also positioned so as to dash that hope immediately, as if to tease and then punish us repeatedly for even imagining that Cordelia, Kent, and the Lear they have loved might possibly survive in Edmund's world. The progression of *King Lear* is only from bad to worse for the sympathetic characters, and this rupture in Shakespeare's practice reflects an imagination actively abstracting the irreversible process by which Edmund's entrepreneurial rapacity becomes historically dominant.

A related feature of *King Lear* is its counterpoint of allegory and realism in representing its characters. Not only Cordelia and Edmund but those aligned with them in their respective sentiments—Kent and Goneril's servant; Goneril, Regan, and Cornwall—are monologic figures, almost allegorical. They enact throughout the play only the sentiments by which they were constituted before the play began, and then within the framework of their static opposition, both Lear and Edgar are dynamically transformed. These two enact within the play a deconstruction (Lear) and reconstruction (Edgar) of personal and political sentiments dialectically linked in a unitary process. Both are stripped of clothing, language, and reason—Lear to mark the death of feudal loyalty represented by his disrobing, madness, and death, and Edgar to mark the bare renewal of life represented by his return to clothing and language for any justice he can find in Edmund's world. Both then bear witness to Edmund's execution of Cordelia, and in thus certifying Edmund's ethics' accession to hegemony, together they complete the play's tragic progression.[24]

These formal departures are both cause and effect of Shakespeare's horrified imagination of capitalist rapacity as represented by Edmund. They are part of a process wherein he reconfigured the family story he found in his source so as to apprehend this one time the history of existing society as a history of class struggle and thus enter into a Marxian imagination.

This imagination has an epistemology of its own in making class its object of knowledge and feeling, and when Jane Smiley restored *King Lear* to its aboriginal form as a family history in *A Thousand Acres*, she withdrew it from this epistemology and returned it to that of *The Dollmaker*. Like *The Dollmaker*'s critique of mass-produced food, *A Thousand Acres* includes some very sharp critiques of capitalist farming, and, also like *The Dollmaker*, it can be read in part as a narrative of capitalism's effect on the family. But that is also to read it as an ethnography of class location rather than a drama of class process with the cognition that that entails. *A Thousand Acres* is often grim and visceral in its fidelity to *King Lear*, but where class is concerned it domesticates *King Lear*.

6

The Marxian narrative of class is produced not only by Shakespeare but also on occasion by other canonical writers, most notably for my purpose Dickens in *Little Dorrit* and James in *The Princess Casamassima*, both like Shakespeare as if in spite of themselves. Dickens's and James's depictions of pristine and alienated labor, of expropriated wealth and poverty in their multiple overdeterminations, also focus the novelistic genre that grew up with capitalism on the same social observation that led Marx to class as an analytic category. And both are the subjects of essays by Lionel Trilling in *The Liberal Imagination* where class and its complexity go unmentioned.

Representing class in its overdetermined complexity was then the goal of some American proletarian novelists of the 1930s and 40s—realist contemporaries of Harriet Arnow in whom we can see the imagination struggling to find an entry through class to the overdeterminations of ethnography. Their struggle mostly failed, and even their successes are more limited than hers. But that their goal remains both viable and necessary can be seen in a contemporary novel like Barbara Kingsolver's *The Poisonwood Bible*, which reflects no less than Dickens and James the Marxian imagination I am trying to identify.

In the remainder of Part One—Chapter Two on Dickens and Chapter Three on the proletarian novelists—I develop more fully the poetics of class outlined in the present chapter. Taken together, Dickens's *Hard Times* and *Little Dorrit* suggest a paradigm for representing class as overdetermined point of entry, and the proletarian novelists' effort to produce this point of entry can be understood most fully in light of Dickens's paradigm. Then in Part Two I address the implications of the poetics of class developed in Part One for, respectively, liberal literary criticism, Marxian social theory, and Marxian cultural theory. Chapter Four develops a Marxian reading of James's *The Princess Casamassima* that challenges the liberal readings of Lionel Trilling and Irving Howe; Chapter Five develops a reading of Meridel Le Sueur's literary career that interrogates Gramsci's theory of hegemony as produced by organic intellectuals; and Chapter Six develops a critique of Raymond Williams and Fredric Jameson as iconic Marxian cultural theorists who, for all their differences, agree in denying the possibility of a Marxian imagination. Where my earlier chapters invoke theory piecemeal to help explicate particular texts, this is the book's one theoretical chapter, and it aims to connect the practical explications of the preceding chapters to Marxian cultural theory at large. Then in Chapter Seven, as a coda, I offer an abbreviated reading of *The Poisonwood Bible* designed to suggest the continuing relevance of its Marxian imagination in today's stunningly ahistorical academic culture.

2

CLASS IN DICKENS FROM *HARD TIMES* TO *LITTLE DORRIT*

When class is understood as a social process rather than an identity site, Resnick and Wolff's linked concepts of overdetermination and point of entry become all but indispensable to explain the representation of class in the novel. Now to develop this explanation further, I want to apply these concepts to two Dickens novels, *Hard Times* and *Little Dorrit*, written consecutively and both depicting their characters' immersion in multiple overlapping social processes at a time when Dickens was consciously confronting class conflict in England. But where *Hard Times* in representing a strike incoherently resists class as point of entry, *Little Dorrit* in representing its family histories coherently adopts it, and this difference goes far to explain the point of entry conditions for representing class in the novel.

Let me emphasize at the outset, however, that I am not proposing overdetermination and point of entry, either singly or jointly, as aesthetic criteria. We can be engaged and enlightened by novels that represent a substantial complexity of overdetermined experience without also "theorizing" this experience through a single point of entry—*Middlemarch*, *Anna Karenina*, *Absalom, Absalom!*—and also by novels with an unmistakable point of entry that requires them to avoid at all cost representing human experience as overdetermined—*Don Quixote*, *Uncle Tom's Cabin*, *To the Lighthouse*. We can remain disengaged or unenlightened by novels whose representation of overdetermined processes arouses little intrinsic interest—*A Hazard of New Fortunes*, *Song of Solomon*—and we can be truly bored by proletarian, feminist, or similarly ideological novels whose compulsive point of entry is unsupported by any credible representation of overdetermined experience—*Middle Passage*, *Surfacing*.

Robert Tressell's *The Ragged Trousered Philanthropists*, "the first working-class novel in English," with its wonderfully acute and excruciatingly detailed representation of worker exploitation in the process of creating, appropriating, and distributing surplus labor, makes class its point of entry and entire ground of apprehension. But although it is admired by people whom I admire, this book can only be stupefying to most readers because almost every detail in its 600 pages is devoted to surplus labor, class dynamics, and nothing else. It removes class from any credible entanglement with the other social processes through which class is dynamically constituted, and I would guess that only political economists already converted can take pleasure in Tressell's novel—and perhaps even then as only modest relief from their famously dismal science.

But if overdetermination and point of entry cannot comprise an aesthetic standard, they can constitute an epistemological project carried out by rhetorical means that parallel the logical means by which a theory like class as process constitutes its epistemological project. The novel's concrete representation of experience explores independently a theory's abstract explanation of that experience and, in so doing, persuades us above all by its rhetorical struggle—when this struggle in fact occurs, as it does in Dickens no less than Shakespeare—either to adopt or to avoid a given point of entry for its represented overdeterminations.

1

Dickens makes a rare and precious example for at least four reasons. First, we can see his struggle in extended display over the course of consecutive novels, *Hard Times* and *Little Dorrit*. Second, he undergoes this struggle as a contemporary of Marx and Engels in responding to the advent specifically in England of what Ellen Meiksins Wood calls *The Pristine Culture of Capitalism*. Dickens was six years older than Marx and eight years older than Engels. *Dombey and Son* (1846–8) is chronologically parallel to *The Condition of the Working Class in England* (1845); *Bleak House* (1852–3) and *Hard Times* (1854) to *The Eighteenth Brumaire* (1852); *Little Dorrit* (1855–7) to *The Grundrisse* (1857), and so forth. So here is an instance of the novelist drawn by his medium to the same task of observation and understanding as the theoretician by his, at just the time and place where capitalism's definitive contours were becoming unmistakably visible. And in these aforementioned novels, as Shaw said of *Hard Times*, "we see Dickens with his eyes newly open and his conscience newly stricken by the discovery of the real state of England."[1]

Third, Dickens is not in the first place a social or political novelist but a prodigy of popular culture whose moment-to-moment invention—verbal, rhetorical, mimetic, narratological—enables him even now to engage all manner of readers for seven and eight hundred pages at a time. At the threshold of this engagement he imparts revolutionary energy to the English language on a scale rarely matched. Then by this language he playfully produces a cornucopia of characters and episodes that answer our desire for our own humanity. Finally, he weaves these characters and episodes into patterned progressions that tickle and surprise us quite irrespective of their political or ideological import.

The deepest pleasure we take in Dickens is like the pleasure we take in Haydn, who was also profusely inventive and affectionately popular, and B. H. Haggin's words about Haydn also apply to Dickens:

> What we hear in Haydn's instrumental music is a constant playing with the medium and with the listener's mind; and sometimes we hear this process raised to incandescence by his exuberance in his use of his powers for that purpose; on every page we get details which it amused him to contrive on Wednesday to startle his listeners, or hold them spellbound, or make them laugh, on Saturday.[2]

In a more resistant medium than Haydn's because it is finally in fact referential, Dickens also plays with our minds and feelings through the wonderful contrivance of his language and episodes. But then in his case also, the referentiality of language drew his spellbinding power and capacity for thought inexorably to politics, to the social and political novel in his development as a popular artist. Any Marxist has to love that.[3]

Fourth, Dickens's later novels, above all *Bleak House*, *Hard Times*, and *Little Dorrit*, actively invite those metaphorical readings which are the built-in reflex of contemporary scholarship and which inexorably mask the narratology of overdetermination by which these novels approach or avoid a possible point of entry. Dickens's figurative language and recurring symbolism are certainly not those of the realist novel anchored in literality. But neither can his ramified web of narrative detail be contained or governed by his metaphors and symbols. There's too much going on in Dickens, and in blinding itself to point of entry as a narrative possibility for organizing what goes on, metaphorical criticism must ignore any representation of class as process. Its own point of entry impels it to regard class as a site when it regards it at all.

Dickens's novels from *Dombey and Son* to *The Mystery of Edwin Drood* maintain his lifelong identification with ordinary people—in the novels and also in their implied audience. They incorporate in their forms his lifelong mixture of picaresque adventures, *Bildung* progressions, histrionic arias, and soap-opera sentimentality and melodrama as typically contradictory, mutually constitutive narratological processes. Then in weaving their completed textures, these novels conspicuously thematize the economics, politics, and culture of capitalist society. All of them are rife with paragraphs of specific denunciation. All link capitalism with patriarchy and represent episodes and sites of capitalist/patriarchal power. And all include rhetorical attacks on capitalist enterprises, institutions, communities, and manners—the Railroad, Chancery, Coketown, Podsnappery.

Only *Little Dorrit*, however, seems to me to produce class as point of entry and ground of apprehension, and I do not think it an accident that *Little Dorrit*'s immediate predecessor, *Hard Times*, is the one Dickens novel in which class conflict and the appropriation of surplus labor are direct objects of representation as in *The Ragged Trousered Philanthropists*. For Dickens's narrative mimesis and progression in *Hard Times* produce a revolutionary theme of class expropriation that threatens to run away with him, and he is moved by a kind of rhetorical anxiety to back off incoherently from the transformative vision threatened by this latent point of entry. Then by a kind of self-overcoming, Dickens finds his way in *Little Dorrit* to a more indirect, less threatening mimesis of class sentiment-become-idea and, through a now coherent narrative progression, to class as point of entry, principle of form, and mimetic ground of virtually Marxian apprehension.

For any number of his own purposes, Karl Marx would love to have written *Hard Times*'s set pieces of condemnation, and so would today's critics of global corporations, free trade agreements, and the World Bank. Here I limit myself with difficulty to quoting only two, yet as many as two in order to suggest something of the extent and power of Dickens's conceptual grasp. The first is the description of Coketown that introduces *Hard Times*'s chief working-class character, Stephen Blackpool:

> In the hardest working part of Coketown; in the innermost fortifications of that ugly citadel, where Nature was as strongly bricked out as killing airs and gasses were bricked in; at the heart of the labyrinth of narrow courts, and close streets upon streets, which had come into existence piecemeal, every piece in a violent hurry for some one man's purpose, and the whole an unnatural family, shouldering, and trampling, and pressing one another to death; in the last close nook of this great exhausted receiver, where the chimneys, for want of air to make a draught, were built in an immense variety of stunted and crooked shapes, as though every house put out a sign of the kind of people who might be expected to be born in it; among the multitude of Coketown, generically called "the Hands"—a race who would have found more favor with some people, if Providence had seen fit to make them only hands, or, like the lower orders of the seashore, only hands and stomachs—lived a certain Stephen Blackpool, forty years of age.[4]

The second is Blackpool's speech to the banker/industrialist Bounderby on behalf of the striking workers:

> "Look round town—so rich as 'tis—and see the numbers o' people who has been brought into bein heer, fur to weave, an' to card, an' to piece out a livin', aw the same one way, somehows, 'twixt their cradles and their graves. Look how we live, an' wher we live, an' in what numbers, an' by what chances, and wi' what sameness; and look how the mills is awlus a goin, and how they never works us no nigher to onny dis'ant object — cepting awlus, Death. Look how you considers of us, and writes of us, and talks of us, and goes up wi' your deputations to Secretaries o' State 'bout us, and how you are awlus right, and how we are awlus wrong, and never had'n no reason in us sin ever we were born. Look how this ha' growen an' growen, Sir, bigger an' bigger, broader an' broader, harder an' harder, fro year to year, fro generation to generation. Who can look on 't, Sir, and fairly tell a man 'tis not a muddle?" (149–50)

I will return to that conclusion about its being a muddle, which is Blackpool's refrain throughout this novel. But the first thing to notice in these passages is their discursive and conceptual analyses of the new economy and politics. While both the narrator in the first passage, and Blackpool in the second, resort on occasion to intensifying metaphors, neither relies on metaphor as an alternative to discursive reasoning in diagnosing the horrrors of capitalism. Both subsume their metaphors to their arguments—"every piece in a violent hurry for one man's purpose," or "never had'n no reason in us sin ever we were born"—and these arguments establish for the reader narrative expectations that ask to be satisfied not metaphorically but conceptually, in and through the working out of the story.

Equally striking in these passages is the eloquence with which Dickens incorporates his politics in the rhythm of his prose—in its balanced parallelisms and antitheses, its iambic beat, its melodic cadences ("sin ever we were born")—and that this prose is so deeply affecting because it is also the vehicle for a multidimensioned conceptual analysis—economic, political, and spiritual—of the damage done to human life by the capitalist class process.

It could be that such prose as this, which I have not read the likes of until Subcommandante Marcos, can be produced specifically within the rhetoric of fiction not by a revolutionary like Marcos but only by a conservative like Dickens who believed in the ultimate unity of class interests but who also cared intensely for common people.[5] That caring in itself may have pushed him to the conceptual understanding embodied in the prose and made him a Marxist in spite of himself, so to speak, in the same way that Engels thought Balzac's depiction of the dynamics of capitalism was deeply congenial to Marxism although Balzac himself was a royalist.

That may be condescending to Dickens and Balzac, but also maybe not. Two class-coded refrains in *Hard Times*, both uncongenial to Marxism, are "What does it matter?" (or "What will be, will be.")—identified with James Harthouse and Louisa Gradgrind until her enlightenment, and "Aw a muddle"—identified with Stephen Blackpool throughout. Louisa's Gradgrindian upbringing produces in her an indifference to her fellow humans, conveyed by "What does it matter?," parallel to James Harthouse's bourgeois/aristocratic indifference as an iconic British "swell." That is one of many damning links between utilitarianism and capitalism in this novel, and it is no accident that Sissy Jupe is the single agent who rescues Louisa from both Harthouse's *ennui* and her own programmed upbringing.

Blackpool's "Aw a muddle," on the other hand, is regularly used to disavow at the last minute the precise, detailed, *unmuddled* analysis and condemnation of capitalism that he himself has just delivered out of concern for his fellow humans—to Bounderby in defense of the striking workers in the passage I have quoted and then to the people assembled for his rescue from the mine pit. Like flustered Melville when he has Ishmael affirm the felicity of wife and fireside in response to joining hands with his fellow sailors in squeezing spermacetti, Dickens cannot follow through on the logic of his own mimesis, and Blackpool's "Aw a muddle" registers Dickens's cop-out.

In performing this cop-out Dickens also resorts to the device of making Blackpool an outcast from his fellow workers no less than from Bounderby. For totally obscure and implausible reasons involving the protection of Rachael, Stephen refuses to join the strikers and thereby earns their rejection; but then immediately following he earns Bounderby's rejection by defending the strikers in the speech I have quoted — a speech whose political detail and revolutionary implications *should* have belonged to the strike leader Slackbridge, who instead is made to spend his eloquence persuading the workers to reject Stephen. (Compare Elia Kazan's calculated cop-outs in his films *On the Waterfront* and *Viva Zapata!*)

This use of Stephen Blackpool to call a plague on both houses, capital and labor, is deeply at odds with Dickens's critique of capital and praise of *unorganized* labor throughout the novel. In this critique and in his portraits of Stephen and Rachael, and even in describing the union meeting, Dickens not only exonerates but idealizes the workers, even "through their very delusions" (139). Their delusion is not about the character or depth of their exploitation, which Dickens has depicted with such accuracy and power, but that they can put an end to their suffering collectively rather than by caring for each other individually, as Louisa finally learns from Sissy to do. Dickens's mimetic muddle can thus be seen as a reaction to the pressure he has put on his form by his devastating critique of capitalism.[6]

After enumerating a myriad of inconsistencies in Dickens's treatment of Stephen Blackpool, Philip Hobsbaum concludes that "Stephen's plot is too wildly biased against him to be representative; it cannot act, therefore, as an expression of the Theme" — and that this explains "the inferiority of this part of Dickens's novel."[7] For all of Dickens's thematic effort to link utilitarianism with capitalism through the character of Bounderby, he remains unwilling to invest Blackpool, as Bounderby's necessary antagonist where capitalism is concerned, with the formal consistency with which he invests Louisa, as Bounderby's necessary antagonist where utilitarianism is concerned. Thus the novel's class plot never gets an equal chance to interact with its utilitarianism plot in a process of rhetorical overdetermination that would reflect a process of social overdetermination while also producing class as point of entry.

Another way to put this might be that a novelist already endowed with Dickens's personal history and concern for ordinary people, coming into the full exercise of his powers at a time when capitalist class processes were becoming discernible to Marx and Engels, pushed himself to the verge of their master narrative and thereby frightened himself into backing off — into deserting his political trajectory in order to maintain his rhetorical balance and customary form. Although the finished novel associates utilitarianism with the ravages of capitalism along the way, it reaches closure by sweeping the strike plot under the Gradgrind plot and then by depicting the redemption of individual Gradgrinds by Sissy Jupe and her circus comrades.

But there is a way in which the two plots can be yoked together—through "the interlocking use of metaphor and metonymy" by which Patricia E. Johnson argues that *Hard Times* reproduces in its own form and structure "the dynamics of capitalist production."[8] Here we can see the difference between a metaphorical apprehension of class as site and a discursive apprehension of class as process enabled by the concept of point of entry. Johnson argues that in representing the destruction of both Louisa and Stephen, *Hard Times* is itself a metonymic capitalist factory in which Dickens "does not provide us with an escape from the system but instead holds us to a strict accounting of what it costs to maintain it" (418). His description of Coketown, where every church, school, hospital, and prison is built on the red-brick model of the factory spewing its smoke, establishes a "metaphorical key-note" (412) for the metonymic relationship between the factory's coke, which is both the fuel that supplies its energy and also the burnt-out residue, and the human lives similarly consumed in Coketown by "the dynamics of capitalist industrial production" (413)—here the lives of Louisa and Stephen, both of whom are associated throughout with images of fire and smoke:

> Superficially, there would seem to be little connection between this older working-class man and this young middle-class woman, but Stephen and Louisa follow the same metonymic pattern. Each begins the novel in a state of confusion, smoke. This is underlined by Stephen's oft-repeated statement that everything is "in a muddle." The connection is strengthened by the fact that both characters' entrapment in the system is manifested primarily in their unhappy marriages. Each, in fact, comes to despise the mate that he or she is tied to for life. Each becomes increasingly isolated from his or her own class or gender, as Louisa seldom returns home after her marriage and Stephen is ostracized by other working-class men for his refusal to join the union. (414)

But for all its metaphorical vividness, the indictment of capitalism produced by Johnson's analysis is obliged to ignore *Hard Times*'s structural ambivalence in condemning the process by which capitalism uses people as fuel. For one thing, Johnson must connect the two characters figuratively by a weak analogy between their unhappy marriages where Dickens is trying to connect them literally through what he conceives as a strong analogy between utilitarianism and capitalism—that both proceed by mathematical calculation rather than human caring. Johnson also ignores the way in which Louisa, who indeed begins in a state of confusion, proceeds to a state of smoke-free clarity when she tells her father (who now "looked a wiser man, and a better man, than in the days ... when he wanted nothing but Facts") that "I will be different yet, with Heaven's help" (209). These utilitarians do not end up as cinders of coke but as reformed vessels of renewable energy.

But Dickens sees no comparable way to rescue Stephen Blackpool for a reformed capitalism, and to sustain her analysis Johnson must ignore Dickens's representation of Stephen as someone who begins *and* ends in a state of perfect clarity about class as process, who moves from an unhappy marriage to a nourishing relationship with Rachael parallel to Louisa's with Sissy Jupe, and who is nevertheless narratologically punished instead of rewarded for his anti-capitalist clarity and self-renewing energy. Stephen is artificially subjected to the falsified refrain, "Aw a muddle," to ostracism by his fellow workers despite his eloquence on their behalf, and then to death not as a working-class hero but simply by accident. The novel does indeed burn him up, but not by way of unmasking metonymically the capitalist system that he himself has unmasked conceptually. It is rather as if Dickens doesn't know where to go with Stephen's unmasking and so must mask *it*, in complicity with rather than in critique of the system.

The contradiction between Louisa's rescue and Stephen's destruction registers Dickens's *avoidance* of "a strict accounting of what it costs to maintain [the system]." It subverts the metonymic pairing of Louisa and Stephen, and it is methodologically obliterated by the metaphorical analysis pervasive in contemporary scholarship. Even a Marxist like Terry Eagleton gets caught in its metaphorical reflex. Writing about Dickens's "self-contradictory forms" in *Criticism and Ideology*, Eagleton says:

> Dickens is forced in his later fiction to use as aesthetically unifying images the very social institutions (the Chancery court of *Bleak House*, the Circumlocution Office of *Little Dorrit*) which are the object of his criticism. It is, ironically, these very systems of confict, division, and contradiction which provide Dickens with a principle of symbolic coherence. . . . It is not that the early Dickens's perception of character as idiosyncratic and non-relational yields to a vision of social unity; it is rather that such non-relationship is now shown to be *systemic*—the function of decentred structures like Chancery, finance capitalism, and the Circumlocution Office.[9]

Eagleton finds as I do "fissures and hiatuses in the text" of the novels that suggest Dickens's hand being forced. But where I find in these fissures a narrative incoherence that reflects Dickens's struggle to resist an emergent point of entry, Eagleton finds them an occasion for Dickens to produce the same "symbolic coherence" of "aesthetically unifying images"—the Chancery of *Bleak House* and the Circumlocution Office of *Little Dorrit*—that Johnson finds in the Coketown of *Hard Times*. Eagleton finds in what he thinks Dickens's failures exactly what Johnson finds in what she thinks his successes, and their agreement suggests how class as point of entry can be masked by metaphorical criticism.

2

This reifying criticism, by virtue of its point of entry, is obliged to treat the integrity of detail in a novel's actual progression as irrelevant. It selects for interpretation only those details that serve its chosen principle of symbolic coherence, ignores the rest, and in effect transforms the novel into a lyric poem monologically stripped of the narratological overdeterminations through which a writer might find a point of entry by telling her entire story. Eagleton says that the Circumlocution Office gives *Little Dorrit* its symbolic coherence, and any number of images and episodes in the novel can be adduced to support his claim. Meanwhile, a veritable army of critics, led by Lionel Trilling, has argued that the Marshalsea Prison gives the novel its symbolic coherence, and even more images and episodes are available to support their claim. Not only does *Little Dorrit* feature literal prison scenes at beginning, middle, and end; its domestic dwellings and human relationships are frequently also shown to be imprisoning—the Clennam mansion, Miss Wade's domination of Tattycoram, Mr. Merdle's enthrallment to commerce. But the experience of imprisonment, as Dickens represents it, is by no means identical with the experience of circumlocution, and the narrative progressions supporting these symbols neither mirror nor metonymize but overdetermine each other. Meanwhile, the novel includes other narrative progressions in which both major and minor characters — Amy Dorrit, Daniel Doyce, John Chivery—refuse from beginning to end either to be imprisoned or circumlocuted. And it is through these characters' sentiments-become-ideas, as Trilling would call them, that *Little Dorrit* weaves its overdeterminations so as finally to make class its point of entry.

Little Dorrit's representation of the capitalist class process is on the one hand less direct than *Hard Times*'s—no factories or strikes—but on the other hand coextensive with the entire novel as a patterned and completed fabric in which pristine labor transcends the class processes of capitalism. It was Dickens himself, in his Postscript to *Our Mutual Friend*, who called the novelist "the story-weaver at his loom,"[10] and *Little Dorrit* is distinctive among his longer novels for its comparatively small cast of characters and its tight interweaving of their stories, which abets the impression that these stories reflect mutually constitutive social processes in the manner theorized by Resnick and Wolff.

The principal interweavings I think are two: of the Merdle and Dorrit family stories and of the individual stories of Daniel Doyce and Amy Dorrit. Several other stories are woven into the pattern made by these pairings—the stories of the Clennam-Dorrit family connection, of Rigaud's role in exposing that connection, of Pancks's career in Bleeding Heart Yard, and of the dynamics of the Circumlocution Office. Several more stories—of Pet Meagles's unhappy marriage and of Miss Wade's domination of Tattycoram—seem to me to function outside the central pattern and yet to reflect social processes (like imprisonment) that help overdetermine the pattern. And then there are stories — of Affery Flintwinch and Flora Finching and John Chivery—that are superfluous to the pattern but are wonderfully gratuitous celebrations of socially constructed humanity.

The two family patriarchs, Mr. Merdle and William Dorrit, are two sides of one bourgeois coin. Their final convergence in the novel, when Dorrit invests his fortune in Merdle's "structures of straw"[11] and is thereby ruined along with Merdle, Clennam, and half of England, closes a connection between them that has been latent throughout. Merdle, who "was in everything good, from banking to building" (246) and who is congratulated by the Lord Treasurer as "one of England's world-famed capitalists and merchant princes" (250), gets no satisfaction from the Society that fawns on him. He is intimidated by his butler, his wife is no more than a showcase for jewels ("You supply manner, and I supply money," he tells her [396]), and at his parties he "was mostly to be found against walls and behind doors" (247), conducting the commercial business that constitutes his whole identity.

William Dorrit, in prison for debt by virtue of the same class process that makes Merdle a merchant prince, constitutes his identity by his social aplomb and is mostly to be found lording it over others while also panhandling as "Father of the Marshalsea." Once he comes into a fortune overnight, Dorrit's sole object is to make his family's manner worthy of the likes of Merdle, and his daughter Fanny finds her identity by marrying Mrs. Merdle's repulsive son simply for the purpose of vanquishing Mrs. Merdle in Society.

Dorrit's windfall and Merdle's ruin have been equally sudden, and in their respective appropriations of surplus labor the debtor has been a social lion and the Midas a social misfit. No social divide keeps their children from marrying, their marriages are motivated entirely by calculation, and the sole aim of their married existence is invidious bourgeois "Society." In all those respects these linked family histories exemplify the famous passage in *The Communist Manifesto* where Marx and Engels explain how capitalism sweeps away "ancient and venerable prejudices" while producing an "uninterrupted disturbance of all social conditions" so that "All that is solid melts into air."

Even so, these family histories represent the *distribution* of surplus labor in a world of manners that is the novel's bread and butter but do not involve any direct representation of the process by which surplus labor is performed and appropriated. There is nothing in *Little Dorrit* comparable to *The Ragged Trousered Philanthropist*'s and *Hard Times*'s representations of actual labor performed and then class conflict between owners and workers. Instead there is at one remove an idealization of work itself, of pristine and productive labor uncorrupted by appropriation, in the linked figures of Daniel Doyce and Amy Dorrit.[12]

Doyce the inventor and small-scale entrepreneur, whose creativity is balked by the Circumlocution Office, can be seen in vulgar Marxist perspective as Dickens's idealization of the *petit bourgeois*. From that perspective Dickens refuses to see how Doyce's enterprise, like Bounderby's in *Hard Times*, must inevitably entail class exploitation irrespective of the Circumlocution Office, so that making a culprit of that office is an evasion comparable to making a culprit of the strike leader Slackbridge in *Hard Times*.

But here that perspective contradictorily helps constitute another perspective, in which Dickens's deliberate vagueness about the nature of Doyce's inventions and enterprise, including the engineering project for which he is called abroad, serves to focus the idealization of Doyce on use-value labor before it is alienated into surplus. Dickens won't tell us specifically what Doyce's work entails because he wants to confine our attention to Doyce's devotion to labor and invention for their own sake. This focus is then sharpened by Dickens's parallel idealization of Little Dorrit throughout the novel.

Amy Dorrit is another Dickensian, patriarchal allegory of female duty and forgiveness, an angel in the house by virtue of her totally selfless devotion to her family and everyone else. But also constituting her allegorical status is her devotion to her needlework, which not only sustains her family financially in debtors' prison but also sustains her spiritually once they become rich. As a beneficiary of new wealth she is an inept student of the foreign languages and society manners which her father hires Mrs. General to teach (and imprison) his children, and amidst the tourist splendors of the Continent she mostly longs for home—even for the Marshalsea Prison. Amidst her family's riches that now make work superfluous, her great freedom is to keep doing for its own sake the work she has always done and to keep remembering the places where she has done it.

In this respect *Little Dorrit* can remind us of Little Eva in *Uncle Tom's Cabin*. In Ms. Stowe's more deliberate allegory, Little Eva is always dressed in white and repeats the refrain, "I'm not nervous, but these things *sink into my heart*."[13] The cause of her fading health is not nerves like her mother's but her perception all around her of Christianity's destruction by racial slavery. At one point she tells Uncle Tom that she can understand why Jesus wanted to die for us because she has felt that way too, yet her death is not that of a Christ figure but of Christianity itself. It cannot survive racial slavery, and when the Holy Spirit expires in the figure of Little Eva, the novel is turned over to the Devil in the figure of Simon Legree.

The difference in their allegories is that Little Dorrit cannot be destroyed by capitalism's class process, as Little Eva is destroyed by slavery's, because the integrity of labor that she represents with Daniel Doyce goes deeper than *any* class process, and here Amy Dorrit can remind us of Frederick Engels alongside Little Eva. Engels argued in *Dialectics of Nature* that labor itself was decisive in the transition from ape to human, and scholars like Stephen Jay Gould have endorsed this argument based on paleontological evidence that upright posture preceded rather than followed the cranial development that differentiates us from our non-human cousins.[14] Upright posture freed the hands for manipulation, manipulation required larger brains, and thus labor became intrinsic to what Marx had called our species being. Amy Dorrit persists in her work long after she needs to make her living by it, and at the end she is sewing curtains for Clennam's prison cell when Daniel Doyce returns to join her in forgiving Clennam and in performing the paternal function by giving her to Clennam in marriage.

This final convergence of Daniel Doyce and Amy Dorrit in rescuing Clennam from Merdle's shipwreck is *Little Dorrit*'s witness to the incorruptible integrity of labor in the face of capitalist expropriation. Their devotion to labor transmutes the Protestant ethic embedded in capitalism into a Marxian ethic of work to reproduce the human community irrespective of the class processes exemplified by Merdle and William Dorrit.

Those class processes are theorized discursively inside the novel by its moustachioed villain, Rigaud, who begins in prison for killing his wife after securing her fortune for himself and who ends by articulating the logic that explains Merdle and Dorrit, Casby and Clennam, Flintwinch and even Pancks, as well as himself. At the novel's penultimate stage its male villain and hero have chiasmically changed places, and Rigaud is asked by Clennam, who is now in prison for investing and losing Doyce's money along with his own in Merdle's fiasco, whether Rigaud sells all his friends. Rigaud replies:

> "I sell anything that commands a price. How do your lawyers live, your politicians, your intriguers, your men of the Exchange? How do you live? How do you come here? Have you sold no friend? . . . Effectively, Sir . . . Society sells itself and sells me: and I sell Society." (749)

Rigaud is the alien whose extravagant behavior unmasks the class process in which the home characters have been enmeshed from beginning to end. He is the return of the repressed, like Balzac's Vautrin, and Lukács's description of Vautrin also applies to Rigaud: "Vautrin's Mephistophelian criticism of the world is only the brutal and cynical expression of what everyone does in this world and of what everyone who wants to survive *must* do."[15]

In the survival world of *Little Dorrit*, the Merdle/Dorrit, Doyce/Dorrit, and Rigaud stories are interwoven throughout and are coextensive with the novel. None is limited to a single site, none is metonymic, and none is animated by a principle of symbolic coherence. They are the mutually constitutive, page-turning preoccupations of a narrative reader from beginning to end, and together these stories make manifest, if not the direct appropriation of surplus labor, the absolute gulf between pristine labor in the figures of Daniel and Amy and the capitalist ravage of appropriated surplus in the figures of all the rest. Who knows but that Shaw had something like this in mind when he said that reading *Little Dorrit* converted him to socialism?[16]

5

The analysis of Dickens's novels I have attempted here, in which class as overdetermined process also becomes rhetorical point of entry, is invited by other novels as well—*The Wings of the Dove*, *The House of Mirth*, the Snopes trilogy. But a list ten times that long would comprise a mere handful where the novel is concerned, and might still seem an insufficient basis for arguing that contemporary narrative theory needs to accommodate a social theory such as Resnick and Wolff's. Yet part of this theory's appeal to me is its Marxian modesty on bourgeois turf, its silent respect for the tremendous range of bourgeois experience represented in most novels that get written—a range of experience it knows it can't explain and ought not try to explain. Just as Resnick and Wolff insist that in the finitude of our lives we are engaged by a variety of mutually constitutive social processes, of which class is only one, we must also insist that not all these identity-producing processes involve exploitation or oppression. Marx himself argued that capitalism, in establishing its process of appropriating surplus labor, enlarged the human spirit in countless ways, and it doesn't take much historical imagination to see around us masses of people who are beneficiaries of this enlargement. At the theater or on the hiking trails, at the school board meeting or the Special Olympics, reading all these novels or even going to the shopping mall, ordinary people of the last two centuries cultivate and express their humanity in dimensions and at depths that could not be dreamed of before the bourgeoisie.

A theory of mutually constitutive social processes, of which exploitative processes of any kind are only a part, has a way to respect the finitude in which all manner of people live upright, fulfilling, and sometimes liberated lives in a world that is also rife with oppression. It has a way to take account of us as individual subjects, and it also has a way to respect the history of the novel itself, which is largely a history of bourgeois celebration. The novel has long been considered an art form of the bourgeoisie, which has to mean in part that as an institutional discourse and signifying practice, the novel is a product of the social leisure created by capitalism's appropriation of surplus labor. Might it be that the praxis of the novel imparts to its practitioners, women and men, black and white, radical and conservative, a vested interest in avoiding class as point of entry? When Dickens's revolutionary insight in *Hard Times* pushed him to break out of that novel's embedding in bourgeois culture, he could no more do it than could Melville in *Moby-Dick* or Brontë in *Wuthering Heights* or Morrison in *Tar Baby*. The late Henry Roth, who was not a communist when he wrote *Call It Sleep*, said that after he became a communist he found himself unable to write fiction that he could find convincing.

Mimetic representation that entails the manners of a latent community may be so deeply embedded in the *status quo* that producing class as point of entry will be not only rare but indirect and inadvertent. I think that happened in *Little Dorrit*, and I think Resnick and Wolff's theory can explain not only the narratology of *Little Dorrit* but also why that narratology must be exceptional within capitalism. Its being exceptional is theoretically significant to a theory that can properly call itself Marxian while also respecting the facticity of bourgeois experience.

The political left in recent years has certainly had reason to lament its impotence. But it has also narcissistically blamed itself for impotence—as if it could have succeeded better if only it could have theorized better—in historical circumstances that constrained it simply to bear witness. Bearing informed witness in the classroom and print venues we have chosen is neither a theoretical nor a practical failure. The Zapatistas for whom Marcos speaks with Dickensian power, in a venue they didn't choose that puts them closer to revolution than any in North America, found their potency by deciding not to risk more at a particular time than just to make waves, and the waves they have made keep seeping even now at the foundations of Mexican society. Just bearing witness or just making waves can be historically appropriate forms of praxis, like revolution itself, that implicate always vulnerable human subjects in deciding how best to attempt anything, and how much is enough, at any given moment of our historical finitude.

For those always vulnerable decisions about what used to be called strategy and tactics, contemporary scholarship too often substitutes the invulnerable reifications of symbolic coherence (with its frequent handmaiden, Foucauldian genealogy). Its praxis is to obscure the constantly changing, often contradictory, mutually constitutive social processes that challenge the judgment of human subjects trying to find their way among those other forms of praxis—in literature as in life. Its practitioners can seldom feel impotent because their metaphors, symbols, and metonymies provide a reified source of self-renewing academic prestige and power. This may also explain a little of the left's sense of impotence. When literary theory appears to keep growing in scope and depth with each new principle of symbolic coherence and the "ism" it entails, why don't we feel better?

The rethought Marxism I am invoking in these chapters offers an alternative to contemporary reification that can reclaim the honor and dignity of humanism. Instead of abandoning that irreplaceable term because of its past appropriations by essentializing elites, this Marxism can rethink humanism as it rethinks itself. It can reclaim for the attention of scholarship and pedagogy a human subject capable of agency and purpose either as woman or man, blackatlantican or mestizo, gay or straight, yet still and all as ardent reader and active citizen.[17] And in again doing that, it can help us recognize processes like class for what they really are.

3

REPRESENTING CLASS IN THE REALIST NOVEL

The novel is friendly in all its forms to the representation of class as identity site: the Gothic novel and symbolic novel, *Bildungsroman* and *Kunstlerroman*, modern, postmodern, and postcolonial novels, all represent class at various locations that reward a Marxian attention. But two forms of the novel share a special affinity with Marxism in their capacity to produce class as holistic point of entry—the utopian novel, which must delineate the class present in order to depict its transcendence in a classless society, and the realist novel, which is not similarly obligated but which grew in the same epistemological soil as Marxism and which aims to depict what Balzac, the acknowledged father of realism writing at the time of *The German Ideology*, called "the cause of these social effects . . . the hidden sense of this vast assembly of figures, passions, and incidents" that comprise society—a society which, thus depicted, would "bear in itself the reason for its working."[1]

The realist novel involves a primarily referential rather than metaphorical storytelling—what David Lodge calls "the representation of experience in a manner which approximates closely to description of similar experience in non-literary texts"[2]—not in the naive faith that this representation literally reproduces social experience but in the sophisticated faith that it produces a reliable model or simulacrum of that experience. Theorists of realism also generally agree, as William W. Stowe puts it, that realism commits itself to the detail of social experience in order to make that experience intelligible and can only make it intelligible by systematizing it in a literary structure which is also informed by the representation of experience in non-literary texts.[3]

Herein lies realism's affinity with Marxism, which commits itself to the detail of experience in order to make that experience intelligible through the dynamics of class. The realist novel is no more committed to class *ā priori* than any other sort of novel, but in its simulacrum of social experience it must open itself to class as other novels may choose not to do, just insofar as class is understood as a process of producing, appropriating, and distributing surplus labor that makes social experience intelligible.

Here again Resnick and Wolff's concepts of overdetermination and point of entry can be hugely instrumental in mapping realism's range of possibilities. Overdetermination is relevant to the realist novel insofar as that novel commits itself to a comprehensive representation of interacting social processes—e.g., printing technology, newspaper financing, and party politics in Balzac's *Lost Illusions*; expatriation, morality, and class in James's *The Portrait of a Lady*; class, race, and gender in Morrison's *Tar Baby*. Then, insofar as overdetermination is already latent in the bread-and-butter representation of the realist novel, the concept of point of entry suggests two further possibilities: a) that any given novel can sort and focus its represented overdeterminations so as to produce a single point of entry, whether class or something else; and b) that this point of entry, if it is produced, can in fact be class.

But these are only possibilities, and at least as often as not the realist novel declines to focus its represented overdeterminations so as to produce any single point of entry. Nor do the cognition, pleasure, or power of the genre depend on its doing so. Thus in a novel like *Daniel Deronda*, the social processes that form Gwendolen Harleth barely intersect, let alone reciprocally determine, those that form Deronda. Or in *Tar Baby*, where Morrison chooses her characters and represents their interactions so as to make the mutual determinations of class, race, and gender unmistakable, none of these emerges as a presiding point of entry overdetermined by the others. In the novel's process and closure that sends Son and Jadine in the directions it does, Morrison is content simply to have represented her overdeterminations.[4] Such examples are not unusual, and the most we can say is that the realist novel's affinity for overdetermination puts it in a favored position both to represent class in a convincing range of overdeterminations and also to make class its point of entry—and, in so doing, to produce a Marxian cognition and power comparable to that produced by other points of entry and other sorts of novel.

But in saying just this much, we come up against the formidable Marxian theory of realism developed by Georg Lukács, a theory which, for all its discrimination and complexity, effectively denies overdetermination while also insisting on class as the sole point of entry, and thus the single criterion of correctness, for the novel. A Marxian address to realism entails an engagement with Lukács, and here I must confine myself to the ways in which a realist theory derived from Resnick and Wolff can provide an alternative to his.[5]

Realism is Lukács's byword and yardstick, and he means by it not only

Lodge's representation of experience that approximates the description of similar experience in non-literary texts, but also a representation of both personal and social experience as wholly determined by the processes of class. For Lukács, the realist novel's characters are implicated in class structures and relations that can only be represented "correctly"—i.e., in accord with "objective reality"—as exclusively governing their society. These characters' actions, however overdetermined, must nevertheless typify their society, so that for the novel representing such characters class is not just one point of entry among the many invited by overdetermined experience. It explains by itself the "totality" of experience and thus precludes the need for other points of entry.

Lukács is everywhere attentive to the realist characters' actions and interactions as a complex interplay of the general and the particular, the internal and the external, the literal and the metaphorical. His distinctions between tendency and partisanship and between reportage and portrayal, along with his conception of the typical and his critiques of naturalism and expressionism, are all aimed at preserving this interplay and keeping the novel as a form free of reification and open to overdetermination. But Lukács then abstracts as typical, and thus as privileged, the class from the nonclass processes in the novel's representation of overdetermined experience. Having insisted theoretically on the conditions of overdetermination, he finesses the fact itself and, in so doing, denies the plurality of partisanships entailed by the concept of point of entry.

His formative 1934 essay on "'Tendency' or Partisanship?" may not sound like that, since it argues for "partisanship" as the realist novel's correct method. But Lukács's partisanship is not that of Resnick and Wolff's chosen point of entry into multiple overdeterminations which cannot be encompassed by a single theory. It is instead a partisanship on behalf of "objective reality with its real driving forces," in which

> there is no space for an "ideal," whether moral or aesthetic. He [the revolutionary writer] does not introduce any demands on the portrayal of reality "from without," for since they are the integral moments of objective reality . . . any demands that grow concretely out of the class struggle are necessarily an inherent part of the writer's portrayal of reality. . . . He does not need to distort the reality, to adjust it or "tendentiously" touch it up, for his depiction, if it is correct and dialectical, is precisely built up on a knowledge of those tendencies (in the proper Marxian sense of the term) that prevail in the objective development. And no "tendency" can or need be counterposed to this objective reality as a "demand," for the demands that the writer represents are integral parts of the self-movement of this reality itself.[6]

The demands that grow out of class struggle are precisely the demands that arise from the objective self-movement of reality itself. They constitute reality, and thus do not require "tendentious" advocacy, whether in the form of a moral ideal or of a chosen (i.e., "aesthetic") point of entry. All they require is transparent portrayal as tendencies in the traditional Marxian sense of objective base and subjective superstructure.

This portrayal is in fact most convincing for Lukács when it contradicts the evident tendentiousness of the novelist himself, as in his favorite examples of Balzac and Tolstoy. Citing Engels on Balzac and Lenin on Tolstoy as points of departure, Lukács plays variations throughout his writing on the contradiction between these two writers' subjective ideals—Balzac's "declining class of the French *ancien régime*" ("Tendency," 40), or Tolstoy's "moral and religious overcoming of this rigid division of society into two hostile camps"[7]—and their objective portrayals of a "class struggle, that lies behind the fetishized forms of capitalist society" ("Tendency," 41). In Balzac, for example, the "demoniacal force" of finance capital, represented by such characters as Gobseck and Nucingen, reaches into every corner of personal and social life:

> Whether the immediate theme is love or marriage, friendship or politics, passion or self-sacrifice, Gobseck is ever present as an invisible protagonist and his invisible presence visibly colours every movement, every action of all Balzac's characters. ("Tolstoy," 145)

And in Tolstoy's lifework,

> the exploited peasant is visibly or invisibly present not only in every greater or lesser phenomenon of life—he is never absent from the consciousness of the characters themselves. Whatever their occupation . . . this occupation and everything human beings think of it, *hinges consciously or unconsciously on problems which are more or less* immediately linked with this central problem. ("Tolstoy," 146; my emphasis)

But these are hugely overstated claims, which Lukács himself in effect concedes by his immediate and immense qualifications of "consciously or unconsciously" and "more or less." In his Tolstoyan example of *Anna Karenina*, for example, the exploited peasant is indeed a presence, both visible and invisible, in the social interactions and personal consciousness of Konstantin Levin ecstatically surveying his fields or talking with fellow landowners about selling forests, improving agronomy, and educating the peasantry. But this same peasant is also rhetorically absent, both visibly and invisibly, from the interactions and consciousness of the other main characters in their happy and unhappy families. Tolstoy's depictions of the Oblonsky, Shcherbatsky, Karenin, and Levin family dynamics, of the Russian military-political bureaucracy in its high-society whirl, of Vronsky racing his horse and Anna sneaking a glimpse of her child—central features of this novel that endear it to generations of readers—may well be depictions of a class society based more or less on some form or other of unseen exploitation. But there is nothing effectively to indicate that this exploitation is specifically of peasants, and meanwhile there is much to indicate that Tolstoy's narrative of overdetermination is concerned no less with the subjection of women than the exploitation of peasants. Lukács's theory requires him to ignore the narrative richness that makes *Anna Karenina* so compelling a novel precisely through its avoidance of class as even a point of entry, let alone as objective reality.

Anna Karenina makes it easy to see how, in the history of classical realism, the representation of class as both overdetermined process and conceptual point of entry has been so rare. Tolstoy's rich invention in portraying overdetermined experience, which led Henry James to call his novels "loose and baggy monsters," resists any apprehension of this experience as determined by a single feature such as class. On the other hand, the realist novel inspired by Marxism that aspires to Tolstoy's richness but that also focuses on class from the outset—including novels that Lukács would honorifically call "partisan" rather than "tendentious"—risks losing its point of entry by representing too fully the loose and baggy overdeterminations of actual experience. If the dominant, mainstream novel too often ignores class or else subsumes it to other determinants, the radical novel too often makes class its point of entry but then conspicuously fails—as if in the spirit of Lukács—to represent a convincing network of overdeterminations in which class and nonclass processes are mutually entangled.

Among mainstream novels, Marxists have regularly argued for Balzac's *Old Goriot*, *The Peasants*, and *Lost Illusions* as comprehensively novels of class. I have argued for Dickens's *Little Dorrit*, which Shaw called "more seditious than *Das Kapital*."[8] The argument can also be made for others—*The Wings of the Dove*, *The House of Mirth*, the Snopes trilogy. Among radical novels, I will be arguing here for Fielding Burke's *Call Home the Heart*, Meridel Le Sueur's *The Girl*, Grace Lumpkin's *To Make My Bread*, and Alexander Saxton's *The Great Midland*. All these novels show it can be done, yet even a much longer list would indicate that it seldom gets done, as if the realist novel's representation of class were constantly under threat even while being enabled. Thus I want to explore in this chapter the realist problematic of class, both in its overdeterminations with nonclass processes and as a point of entry for these overdeterminations.

1

Let me turn as a preliminary to a pair of strange bedfellows—Henry James and the late Henry Roth—who suggest summarily between them the difficulty involved in producing class as point of entry. In *The Princess Casamassima* (1886), to which I will turn in detail in Chapter Four, James made what his critics consider his most deliberate attempt at a realist novel in the tradition of Balzac, and he took for his subject the revolutionary movement whose mostly anarchist agitations and assassinations were familiar London newspaper items at the time he was writing. But while *The Princess* finally makes class its reluctant point of entry, it does so not primarily by external documentation in the manner of Balzac but by internalizing its hero's conflict between his prior commitment to revolution—he has sworn to perform an assassination when called upon—and his growing awareness of European "art, literature, and history"[9] that he comes to believe revolution would destroy.

As Hyacinth Robinson's conflict develops, he comes to say of Diedrich Hoffendahl, the anarchist leader to whom he made his oath, that "he wouldn't have the least feeling for . . . incomparable abominable old Venice. He would cut up the ceilings of the Veronese into strips, so that everyone might have a little piece. I don't want everyone to have a little piece of anything and I've a great horror of that kind of invidious jealousy which is at the bottom of the idea of a redistribution" (1:147).[10] Yet a hundred pages later he can still think of "the flood of democracy" (i.e., revolution, for James) as a "high healing uplifting tide," which, if it does succeed in covering the world, will have only itself to blame "if want and suffering and crime should continue to be ingredients of the human lot" (2:262–3). This double sense of revolution's healing potential and historical accountability keeps Hyacinth committed to his oath despite his terrible reservations; his conflict then immobilizes him just like Hamlet, to whom James compares him in the novel's Preface; and he ends by committing suicide. By rhetorically honoring Hyacinth's socialism equally with his "art, literature, and history," James represents the political activist's equivalent to a writer's conflict between producing class as point of entry and writing a novel at all.

Henry Roth was not a Communist when he published *Call It Sleep* to critical acclaim in 1934, then stopped writing for thirty years after he became a Communist in 1936, and in a 1968 letter tried to explain what had happened:

> My novel was a kind of carry-over, was conditioned by a previous apolitical, a-economic (if not anti-), semimystical decade espousing art for its own fair sake. In short, it was, or was

> akin to, an atavism. And as soon as I realized this "fact," as soon as the realization of my noncommitment smote me, as soon as I grappled with commitment, I became immobilized . . . Allegiance once deeply inhaled was as lethal as carbon monoxide, and as inseparable from fancy's bloodstream.[11]

Roth wrote elsewhere as if this conflict between political allegiance and the writer's bloodstream were an accident of temperament peculiar to him, and in fact we can see that his Joycean lyricism in *Call It Sleep* might not be immediately suited to a representation of class. But the virtual congruence between Roth the radical's pained self-analysis and James the conservative's tragic mimesis suggests that this may not be a personal matter. It raises a question whether the awareness that might lead the novelist to class as point of entry doesn't also meet an endemic resistance that helps explain why novels of class are so rare.

2

What, whence, and wherefore this resistance? One litmus test for both mainstream and radical novelists is the direct representation of workers and their work under capitalism, which more often than not takes the form of a strike novel. A strike calls irresistible attention to class by mainstream novelists like Dickens who are also genuine thinkers. Even the temporary and partial breakdown of capitalism signaled by a strike can make them question what's been happening all along. A strike also offers proletarian novelists like Mary Heaton Vorse or Fielding Burke the chance to represent, in addition to the class process they already know about, the strikers' new experience of solidarity that is a foretaste of the experience of classlessness.

But even the conditions of the strike novel more often than not fail to produce a convincing representation of class as point of entry. Here we can recall the failure of Dickens's *Hard Times* to integrate its two-pronged attack on Benthamite education and capitalist exploitation in the character of Bounderby. Where Dickens enables Louisa Gradgrind to outgrow both Bounderby and her Benthamite upbringing, he balks at imagining a similar progression for Stephen Blackpool, whom he makes implausibly decline to join the strike while the strike leader Slackbridge incredibly denounces him, on the way to frittering away his strike plot by killing off Blackpool and bringing the novel to closure on the redemption of the Gradgrinds. The effect of all this is both a) to cut off the representation of class from its possible overdeterminations with nonclass processes like utilitarian education, and b) to ensure that class will not in any case become *Hard Times*'s point of entry.

Dickens's success and failure in *Hard Times* have their own historical specificity. Marxists have regularly praised Balzac for representing the ruthless dynamic of capitalism despite his own politics. But Balzac was a royalist, and his representation of capitalist processes was rooted in Raymond Williams's "residual" culture of the pre-Revolution aristocracy. Dickens's politics were what we would call conservative but also now were rooted in Williams's "dominant" culture of the bourgeoisie, so that his abhorrent representation of Bounderby and sympathetic representation of Blackpool really bear witness against his own class. The intensity of his outrage and sympathy may then have pushed his class allegiance to the edge of an abyss from which he had to pull back by excising his strike plot and ending his novel on familiar terrain.

3

The radical novelist begins on the other side of that abyss, committed in advance to the proletariat as a class, yet also now groping on unfamiliar terrain for Williams's "emergent" culture of classlessness implied by that commitment. Here too the strike novel is a litmus test, and here we find the radical novelist often bypassing the representation of overdetermination just as the mainstream novelist bypassed point of entry.

Almost the full range of possibilities for the radical strike novel is represented by the four novels by women inspired by the 1929 textile strike in Gastonia, North Carolina. Besides the history of the strike itself, these novels share common factual material for their fictional representations—for example, that the mill hands had been poor but independent hill farmers imbued with both old-time religion and the custom of settling their disputes by violence; that men deserted their wives and children when discouraged by unemployment; or that women were crucial to radical consciousness-raising, both in performing their dual role as workers and childbearers and in challenging their men's racism by including black workers in their movement.

Mary Heaton Vorse's *Strike!* (1930) subsumes this kind of material as background to the strike, whose day-to-day drama included not only picketing, scab labor, and the National Guard with tear gas and bayonets, but also housing evictions and a tent city, the destruction of strike headquarters by company thugs, the murder of a woman strike leader, a sheriff killed in a gun fight, and a trial and acquittal of strike leaders. All this is capable of being narrativized to produce absorbing suspense, and *Strike!* often reads like a thriller. But for that to happen, its concern with class as a process of expropriation must be marginalized to conversations where a strike leader discourses on that topic in response to a reporter's questions.

Another novel that tells instead of shows where class is concerned is Myra Page's *Gathering Storm* (1932). Or more precisely, the contrived situations and cardboard characters by which Page thinks to produce a mimesis of class are melodramatically gross, structurally incoherent, and rhetorically limp. As if the factual material I've summarized weren't already enough, in this novel a whole black family is lynched or murdered *en masse*, and in the very next chapter their surviving brother in New York is arrested and beaten for attending a Eugene Debs rally. A U.S. Army deserter jumps in front of a train, a woman comrade moves to Russia and is elected to the Moscow City Council, and the southern mill worker heroine is sent *Wage-Labor and Capital* by her brother up north, who then comes home to help organize the strike and finds his sister's water supply poisoned by company agents. Page feels compelled to deliver knockout blows on every topic of radical concern, and her novel reads like a caricature of proletarian realism.

The two Gastonia novels that produce class as point of entry through its mutual determinations with other social processes like gender and religion are Fielding Burke's *Call Home the Heart* (1932) and Grace Lumpkin's *To Make My Bread* (1932). Both spend roughly their first halves depicting the economy, agronomy, and livelihood, along with the religion, music, and mysticism, of the mountain farmers before they are driven to the mill towns by predatory lumber companies or by their own desire for their children's schooling. Then both novels represent through direct mimesis the appropriation of surplus labor in the mills as well as the workers' victimization in the mill towns by furniture dealers, loan sharks, doctors, and ministers. Both represent the overlap and sometimes conflict between the workers' growing class consciousness and their growing feminist consciousness, and also a conflict between their new class militancy and their once sustaining religion and music of resignation. In one episode two novice women mill hands learn that the word "stock" refers not to cattle but to making money without working for it; in another a novice woman mill hand is awed like Henry Adams by the power of the machine even as she senses that her skill as an operator will be used to create a speed-up for her fellow workers; in another a woman is positively relieved when her husband, who had become "almost worthless," deserts her and the children; and in several episodes well-meaning ministers are shown losing their authority over newly militant parishioners for whom religion was formerly an opiate.

In dramatizing the mutual determinations of these and other elements in the lives of their characters, Burke's and Lumpkin's novels also produce very often a resonant, nuanced prose instead of Vorse's and Page's documentary flatness.

The documentary style is invited by the strike itself, and in Vorse's thriller devoted entirely to the strike this style is functionally appropriate. But in the other three novels it frustrates any convincing mimesis of the process of overdetermination through which class might become a persuasive point of entry.[12] In them the strike is simply a result of this process, and finally it seems as if class becomes a convincing point of entry in *inverse* proportion to the space these novels devote to the strike. In the caricature of Page's *Gathering Storm*, the strike occupies 191 pages out of 374, or roughly one-half; in Burke's *Call Home the Heart* it is 111 pages out of 434, or one-fourth; in Lumpkin's *To Make My Bread* it is 50 pages out of 384, or one-eighth; and Burke's and Lumpkin's are the two Gastonia novels that have been thought worthy of reprinting in the feminist/left revival of recent years.

At one point in Vorse's *Strike!* the union organizer explains to the reporter how the unionized mountain people-turned-mill workers regard the union as if it were a church in which you attain salvation simply by becoming a member. He is trying to dissolve this reification by cultivating an ongoing activist solidarity, and a hundred pages later a striker's experience of solidarity is described as follows:

> Dewey felt this. He couldn't have explained it in words. He only knew that he was amplified. That he was more alive at this moment than he had ever been, and that everywhere about him people were alive like him.[13]

In a related passage in Burke's *Call Home the Heart*, after its heroine Ishma has committed to the union and is secretly organizing on the shop floor, she is described as follows:

> She was upheld by that supreme ecstasy, the consciousness of transmuting daily life into an ideal. She was part of the creative gesture, building a brighter world; a world so near that she could stretch her hands over the border and feel them tingling with its sun. The dry bread she ate at Mildred's table was sweet with life to come.[14]

Such passages are not in the traditional sense utopian but in Raymond Williams's sense "emergent"; they are the realist novel's representation of a concrete historical experience many of us have had on picket lines, an experience that hints at one dimension of life in a classless society.[15]

But this experience is also ecstatic and transient in our everyday life in a class society.[16] It is very likely an experience Dickens could not have imagined for all his eloquence in denouncing capitalism, but it is also for now an experience too fragile to support an extended, convincing representation of its overdeterminations. By the end of *Call Home the Heart*, Ishma has withdrawn from union activity and gone back to the hills, where her still radicalized and still overdetermined life becomes the subject of a repetitive sequel (*A Stone Came Rolling*), and here perhaps we come to the end of what the strike novel can show us about an emergent structure of feeling.

Insofar as that novel depends on a representation of Williams's "dominant" society that is broad enough and deep enough to reveal this society's need for transformation, it is pulled back toward common ground with the mainstream novel. For the radical novel seems to succeed best when it represents the process of radicalization as one in which many elements besides class affect people's lives—including sports or religion or music—that don't immediately involve exploitation, and in which the transcendence of exploitation is brief and fleeting. But in that case it would also appear that the mainstream novelist has an advantage over the radical novelist in reaching this depth of engagement, since she is unreservedly immersed in and committed to the dominant culture whose overdeterminations provide her fictional material. The radical novelist has one foot in and one foot out of this culture, and insofar as she reaches beyond the dominant culture's overdeterminations to imagine an emergent culture, she can be distracted as a novelist precisely by her opposition. Might it be that Dickens's representations of capitalist class processes are so conceptually powerful and rhetorically moving simply because Dickens's allegiance to capitalism remains undivided despite his devastating critique?

4

Insofar as the human unity produced by a strike is more often than not evanescent, the strike novel must remain for the radical novelist a more limited form than it might at first appear. She must eventually go on to imagine a concrete source of historicized allegiance beyond the unity produced by a strike, and to illustrate the further struggle this entails, let me turn finally to Alexander Saxton's *The Great Midland* and Meridel Le Sueur's *The Girl*, both of which strive to produce class as point of entry while also representing an emergent culture of classnessness that is itself more fully overdetermined, and thus more sustaining, than the evanescent solidarity produced by a strike.

Both are remarkable novels in more ways than I can specify here. Saxton takes as his subject the lives of already converted communists—white and black, men and women—not in their transient epiphanies but in their everyday grubbiness and grind. He depicts their efforts in 1940–41 to organize Chicago railcar repairmen and in that process to combat co-opted and racist union leadership, to support strikers in an adjacent canning factory, and to conduct evening classes in Marxist education while also participating in their families and teaching the neighborhood kids to play football.

In its detailed representation of railroad car maintenance as a labor process, of the workers' hours and exposure to weather and accident, of their demonstrations, union meetings, and CP meetings, and of company cops and thugs, *The Great Midland* clearly makes class its point of entry, and the elegant precision of its affectionate mimesis is often in itself powerfully moving. The following passage, for example, is not only Balzacian in its atmospheric detail; it also evokes the integrity of a labor process on behalf of which the novel's communists devote their lives to improving the conditions and rewards of work:

> The engineer on the switch engine blew three blasts of his whistle. Dave ran up the platform and swung himself into the engine cab. With a deafening roar of steam the pop-off valve let go, and the fireman wrestled with his injector to get more water into the boiler. Dave shouted into the engineer's ear, "I want to drop off at Andrews Street. Will you slow down under the viaduct?" The engineer nodded and Dave, stepping across the cab, sat down on the opposite seat box to keep out of the fireman's way. The engine puffed slowly backwards now, while the fireman stoked his boiler against the drag of the coaches they were pulling out of the depot. The fireman worked with a steady swing, scooping coal from the bunker behind him, then with a long sweep of his shovel, driving the coal into the roaring fire. The engineer leaned back on his throttle, the engine barked against the load, while the floor plates buckled and crashed under the fireman's feet. At each swing of the shovel and each opening of the butterfly doors, a red glare of heat swirled out into the cab. The fireman wiped his face with his bandanna.[17]

A passage like that, of which there are several in *The Great Midland*, represents labor as worthy in and for itself—unlike, say, Zola's *Germinal* or Sinclair's *The Jungle* or the Gastonia novels, where labor is luridly represented only as exploitation—and its tactile evocations and rhythms will be lost on those who have persuaded themselves that language cannot be referential.

Yet for all that, *The Great Midland* threatens to become monochromatic without adequate representation of nonclass processes overdetermining its class processes, and Saxton anticipates this difficulty in depicting the fractious marriage of his two main characters, Dave Spaas and Stephanie Koviak. Dave, who in their childhood musings talked about becoming an engineer, has grown up instead to fight in Spain and then become a communist "carknocker" (i.e., railcar repairman) spending all his off-hours on political organizing. Stephanie, a carknocker's daughter who in childhood was inspired by her visits to the Art Institute, has grown up to be a graduate student in comparative anatomy, and when the novel opens she is living with a graduate student in philosophy after having separated from Dave when he chose to fight in Spain.

Stephanie and Dave reenact their union and separation during the novel, and here Saxton genders his overdeterminations in the form of Stephanie's conflict after she becomes a communist, between the exclusive commitment represented by Dave and an inclusive, virtually Jamesian commitment to art and science as well as politics represented by her life at the university (where her brother and his sometime partner, for example, are pursuing academic careers in Old French).

In his Introduction to the new edition, Saxton says that in writing the novel he identified consistently with Stephanie but that his 1948 readers thought Stephanie "embodied bourgeois hang-ups" (xx) and praised instead his portrait of Dave as "a 'believable' communist hero." Meanwhile, "readers since the 1970s have favored Stephanie over Dave, and it is largely due to Stephanie that *The Great Midland* is being republished" (xix).[18] If he had to defend Stephanie today, Saxton says,

> I would begin by saying that class cannot encompass the entirety of human experience. In a curious way this is like saying that mimesis, or reportage, by itself cannot encompass a whole work of art. (xx)

Here Saxton voices a Resnick–Wolff thesis that class as point of entry, when abstracted from its relations with nonclass processes, can become the subject only of reportage and not a whole work of art. Yet in a crucial respect *The Great Midland* fails to make this thesis narratologically convincing. Although Stephanie's conflict gives the novel a parallel drama to its central drama of interracial labor organizing, Saxton does not allow her private conflict to affect that public drama. Stephanie may be dynamically overdetermined, but she is denied any influence on unshakeable Dave, who at one point explains himself by telling her, "You must want one thing most of all, Stephanie" (312). Their divergence, moreover, is not developed until the final 60 pages of a 300-page novel, after everything essential to its class/race solidarity story has been substantially told. As a result, Stephanie can't help sounding often in their fights like a henpeck whose husband is spending his nights bowling instead of organizing. Stephanie in her overdeterminations is kept from influencing Dave, and her story is timed so as to avoid any overdetermining influence on Dave's and Pledger McAdams's center-stage story of interracial communist activism. Rhetorically speaking, overdetermined

Stephanie is too nearly marginalized, and this leaves class too nearly underdetermined as the novel's point of entry.

Saxton's personal identification with Stephanie and his theoretical conviction that class can't encompass all human experience were thus finally insufficiently enabling. Even in a novel as accomplished as *The Great Midland*, what he felt to be the demands of his Dave/Pledger story continued to preclude a functional interweaving of Stephanie's story with theirs that would make fully convincing the overdeterminations he prized in identifying with Stephanie.[19] It is hard to imagine a more persuasive example of the radical writer's difficulty in producing for the realist novel a Marxian combination of overdetermination and class as point of entry.

Where *The Great Midland* imagines an emergent society in the everyday bonding of its communist organizers, Le Sueur's *The Girl* imagines the bonding of women through childbearing and mothering in a commune whose very existence entails opposition to the bourgeois welfare system. And where *The Great Midland* evinces signs of narratological struggle by gendering its overdeterminations in the character of Stephanie Koviak, *The Girl* struggles to make gender join class, rather than displace it, in a single point of entry.

The Girl is a *Bildungsroman* narrated by its eponymous heroine, who begins as a sexually innocent, gender-innocent, class-innocent waitress in a restaurant that also fronts for a bootleg speakeasy. Her influences there are Clara, the other waitress who moonlights as a whore and dreams of a Norman Rockwell marriage; Belle, who owns the restaurant with her husband Hoinck, whom for years she has rescued from scrapes with the law in between abortions and beatings; Amelia, a midwife and leader of the Workers Alliance whose husband was killed in a strike after telling her "he'd rather die fighting than be a scab or live like a mouse";[20] and along with these very different women an undifferentiated assortment of men who are trying to get leverage on life in the Depression by bootlegging, scabbing, and bank robbing while also subjecting their women to an endless cycle of drink, sex, abortion, and beating.

Their story is told in three segments. First, the Girl imbibes the herstories of Clara and Belle, and in so doing exemplifies Le Sueur's oft-stated claim that the writer's function is to record the voice of the people. In an Afterword she says that *The Girl* is based on actual women's stories which she took down and collected, and her heroine as nameless naif is meant in part as a transparent medium for those stories:

> I listened about men from Belle while I wandered with Clara. Clara's been twice to the house of correction and she says you learn a lot about how not to get screwed there. Belle says this is a rotten stinking world and for women it is worse, and with your insides rotting

> out of you and men at you day and night and the welfare workers following you and people having to live off each other like rats. It's covered with slime, she says. I wouldn't bring up no kids in it. She says she had thirteen abortions. (10)

She proceeds despite all this to her love affair with Butch, to whom she feels magnetically attracted even if his creed is "You got to be tough and strong alone" when, as she tells him, "I don't want to be alone. I want to be with others" (17). Butch has been a miner and machine assembler at 70 cents an hour; now he guiltily scabs and dreams of getting money to lease a gas station and settle down with her; and when she follows him bleeding out of a foul hotel after her very first sexual experience, she says, "I came out of that hotel as out of the hole of hell but also the meadows of heaven" (53).

In the second segment the now pregnant Girl refuses an abortion despite the urgings of Clara and Butch, while Butch, Hoinck, and the other men plan a bank robbery in which the Girl is to drive the getaway car. When the robbery is disrupted in progress and the robbers fatally shoot each other, she drives off with the wounded Butch, and when they stop for gas they hear from the proprietor how leasing a gas station is just another form of capitalist peonage. Then Butch dies in dawning political enlightenment.

It is the novel's final segment that has attracted most attention and been interpreted to encompass the whole. Here the Girl returns to a circle of women—Clara, Belle, Amelia, and now others as well—gathering to form a commune in an abandoned warehouse. But first she seeks help from the relief agencies and is put in a psychiatric hospital where she is slated for sterilization once her child is born. She is then rescued by Amelia the activist midwife, who also organizes a demonstration outside the relief office demanding milk and iron pills for pregnant women. Meanwhile the relief agencies have subjected Clara to shock treatments, and she is brought to the commune to die just as Amelia delivers the Girl's baby—a girl she names Clara—flanked on one side by the dead Clara and on the other by the Workers Alliance mimeograph machine, "sitting in the middle of the floor as if it were some kind of shrouded altar" (141).

The Girl's final apotheosis of motherhood has been anticipated by such earlier statements as Amelia's "you will have a child and then you will belong to the whole earth" (112), and it has been rhetorically enabled by having the novel's men kill each other out of greed for the spoils when their robbery is disrupted. All this certainly invites the conclusion that here gender has displaced class, deliberately and explicitly, as the novel's now exclusive point of entry.

Yet there are many signs that Le Sueur has been trying all along to hold on to class in its overdeterminations with gender and produce a point of entry in which both inflect each other. As the gathering of women around the birthing Girl proceeds, some strikingly alien notes are struck. The mourning Belle says of Hoinck, by whom she had thirteen abortions and even more beatings:

> "Yes sir, when Hoinck pawned his tools that was the end of us all. What tools is to a man. He pawned his tools, he pawned more than his tools. He pawned his skill, being able to do something that gives a man pride. What can a man do without tools? He has to lick the boots of crazies like Ganz. (137-8)

And in her funeral oration for Clara, Amelia says,

> Clara never got any wealth. . . . She never stole timber or wheat or made poor flour. She never stole anyone's land or took it for high interest on the mortgage. She never got rich on the labor of others. (146)

In passages like these, as in that symbolism of the mimeograph machine as a shrouded altar, women become historical subjects not only through "female" desire but also through a "male" class consciousness intertwined with it.[21] In that process, gender and class push to combine in a single point of entry.

But such passages are arrestingly discordant in these final pages, even if they are perfectly logical extensions of much that has come earlier. Amelia, the wonder-working organizer and midwife, was married, after all, to a man who would rather die fighting than scab, and Butch felt embarrassed at scabbing, refrained from imposing on the Girl sexually until she decided she was ready, joined in the robbery so as to get his gas station and begin a life with her, and then died raving in a dawning class consciousness. Until they were killed off, these men were in mutually overdetermined relations with the women, and, just as the Girl felt she'd been in the meadows of heaven as well as the hole of hell after her first lovemaking with Butch, when she finally bears his child we get a passage like this:

> Breathe, Amelia kept saying, wait—push—stop—breathe. He asked me before he died, Do we belong to the human race? Some people think we don't, I said, but we do. Yes we do. This is your face, Butch, coming back down the great river, the great dark. I was bucking like a goat, lifting like a mountain. I heard the mimeograph start. A kind of beat.
>
> It's crowning, Amelia said, I never had heard that. . . . O girl it's coming, easy now. I felt all the river broke in me and poured and gave and opened. Was it my cry, the cry of the women, the cry of a child? The last breath of Butch, the first of a child. (147)

So it was everybody's cry of birth—Butch's no less than the Girl's, the women's, and the child's—not to mention that mimeograph machine. Here again Le Sueur is trying to pick up and interweave the thread she dropped earlier in eradicating the men, a thread of heterosexual love encompassing "male" class consciousness which her feminist trajectory impelled her to mute in the novel's final section.

Thus in obverse ways Saxton and Le Sueur both struggle to combine class with gender in a single point of entry to Marxism's master narrative. Saxton, despite his "cross-gendered" identification with Stephanie Koviak, is still laggard in making Stephanie's overdeterminations impact class as his point of entry; Le Sueur, despite her "cross-gendered" sympathy with Amelia's husband and Butch, is also laggard in making their class struggle impact gender as her point of entry. Both writers visibly strive to combine overdetermination with class as point of entry, and both are visibly too sporadic or too late.

5

Their successes and failures, like those of Dickens, James, and the Gastonia novelists, have their own historical specificity. Dickens represented class as a process of surplus appropriation while also denying it mutuality with nonclass processes. James gave it that mutuality, but strictly as a source of personal tragedy for his protagonist. The Gastonia novels clearly make class their point of entry and, since the martyred leader of the Gastonia strike was also a woman, show no sign of strain in making women as well as men the subjects of class consciousness. But the Gastonia novels can only represent the transcendence of gender and class as ecstatic and transient, so that Saxton's and Le Sueur's effort to concretize this transcendence in the overdetermined immediacies of everyday life is just the struggle we should expect from the left in the 1930s and 40s.

The Great Midland and *The Girl* are "post-strike" novels insofar as their class and gender solidarities are already achieved and must now be sustained day by day. Sustaining them required a fresh address to what the CPUSA called "The Woman Question," which it had long repressed in deference to class, and in addressing this question in their different ways, Saxton and Le Sueur both were hard pressed to connect gender with class in a single point of entry. The realist novel's capaciousness, which invited their effort, also accommodated its failure, and that raises a question whether the representational resistance I have been suggesting all along is finally not in the realist medium but in the radical novelist's message of an emergent structure of feeling.

Don't we come back here again, as in the Gastonia novels, to a gap between that novelist's theoretical commitment and her fund of concrete experience to draw on? The women's commune of *The Girl*, suggested by the actual commune Le Sueur helped establish in St. Paul, is markedly more "emergent," in embodying a sustainable structure of feeling, than the class solidarity ecstasies of *Strike!* and *Call Home the Heart*. But Le Sueur's desperately abbreviated representation of this commune, as in the passages I have cited, reads more like a utopian allegory than a realist mimesis—as if she had to force her material in the absence of observable experience. Either that experience did not yet exist in sufficient density to be represented in the realist mode, or else even so committed a realist could not find her way to represent it. But that is another story, social and political no less than rhetorical, to which I will return in Chapter Five with an analysis of Le Sueur's entire career. Here the present story must conclude simply by observing that the realist mode, hospitable as it is to a representation of class in its overdetermined complexity, entails risks proportionate to its opportunities. It is not *ipso facto* a Marxian mode in the way Lukacs claimed but simply a more capacious mode in which to actively cultivate, as Shakespeare and Dickens also cultivated in their modes, a Marxian imagination.

PART TWO

Some Consequences for Critical Theory and Practice

4
"SOCIALISM-ANXIETY": *THE PRINCESS CASAMASSIMA* AND ITS NEW YORK CRITICS

In 1848 *The Communist Manifesto* began by describing communism as "a spectre haunting Europe," and now 150 years later Aijaz Ahmad describes socialism as "the emancipatory desire of our epoch."[1] During the historical transition marked by those two phrases, millions of people everywhere (except possibly North America) have recognized the spectre and personally felt the emancipatory desire. In so doing, many have had to pass from one anxiety to another—from that of a threatened bourgeois to that of an expectant socialist. The first anxiety is addressed by the *Manifesto*, whose avowed purpose is to explain how communism seeks only to eliminate capitalism's "conditions of oppression." But it is by now a truism that Marx and Engels are more compelling as critics of capitalism than theorists of socialism, and meanwhile, ever since they wrote, the historical failures of existing socialism have only served to dramatize the second anxiety over socialism's capacity to fulfill the emancipatory desire it arouses.

Henry James's *The Princess Casamassima* (1886) represents both anxieties with an exceptional generosity of imagination. Among the few overtly political novels produced in a great age of fiction, *The Princess* stands alone (as far as I know) in honoring socialism as its protagonist's desire and then in producing a classical tragic conflict involving that desire. Where Dostoevsky and Conrad in their political novels manifest the exclusive anxiety of a dominant culture threatened by socialism, James in his inclusiveness juxtaposes with that an emergent anxiety over socialism's future. His hero is torn between an allegiance to the "art, literature, and history,"[2] that he comes to fear socialism will destroy, and an allegiance to "the flood of democracy . . . rising over the world," in a "high healing uplifting tide," which he comes to believe will have only itself to blame "if want and suffering and crime should continue to be ingredients of the human lot"

(2:262–3). Finally unable to resolve this conflict, he commits suicide, and in the New York Preface to the novel written with twenty years' hindsight, James compares Hyacinth Robinson with Hamlet and Lear as someone "finely aware and richly responsible" (1:viii) in living his tragedy.

The Princess is also revealingly fissured, I will argue, in response to the rhetorical pressure of its reluctantly honorific representation of socialism. Then I will argue that its respect for socialism is just as revealingly ignored by the "New York Intellectuals" who chose to write about this novel. In their very different ways, Lionel Trilling in *The Liberal Imagination* and Irving Howe in *Politics and the Novel* finesse *The Princess*'s homage to socialism in the process of distancing themselves from the Marxism of their contemporaries. Where James in honoring socialism was impelled to recognize class as a "master narrative" of modern history and thus to share common ground with Marx and Engels, the New Yorkers' dissent from Marxism entailed rejecting its master narrative and removing class from their generation's agenda. By ignoring James's prescience in giving socialism even a semblance of its historical due, they repositioned him as essentially a moral psychologist for a new generation already on its way to what Ellen Meiksins Wood calls *The Retreat from Class* characteristic of contemporary scholarship.[3] Thus I hope here not only to recover James's precocious achievement but also to show how class has become for so much recent scholarship the lip-service afterthought to gender and ethnicity simply because, as James's achievement can suggest, class in any functional sense is finally inseparable from Marxism's master narrative.

1

In his 1907 Preface to the New York Edition, James recalls *The Princess*'s gestation with impassive assurance. He says that from his long habit of walking the streets, Hyacinth Robinson "sprang up for me out of the London pavement" as "some individual sensitive nature . . . capable of profiting by all the civilisation, all the accumulations to which [the London streets] testify, yet condemned to see those things only from outside—in . . . mere wistfulness and envy and despair." His envy and despair lead him to adopt "an aggressive, vindictive, destructive social faith," and for his story to arouse "pity and terror" it was then only necessary "that he should fall in love with the beauty of the world, actual order and all, at the moment of his most feeling and most hating the famous 'iniquity of its social arrangements'" (1:xvi–xvii).

All this sounds as if he was fully in command of a classical tragedy at the time he sat down to write. But in the tragedies to which James compares his, Hamlet and Lear arouse pity and terror by confronting two moral positions between which there is no easy choice, and the conflict between a love of worldly beauty and a vindictive social faith whose substance is mocked by inverted commas is not that sort of conflict. The beauty of the world will trump vindictiveness every time, and there can be neither pity, nor terror, nor even much engaging suspense in watching it do that.

Yet James's condescension to socialism in the retrospect of the Preface is not what informs his novel, and neither is his implication in the Preface of having been in command of his subject from the beginning. Here is his notebook entry for August 10, 1885, a month before *The Princess*'s first installment was to appear:

> It is absolutely necessary that at this point I should make the future evolution of *The Princess Casamassima* more clear to myself. I have never yet become engaged in a novel in which, after I had begun to write and send off my MS., the details had remained so vague.... The subject of *The Princess* is magnificent, and if I can only give up my mind to it properly—generously and trustfully—the form will shape itself as successfully as the idea deserves.[4]

He was feeling his way at the time far more than he later acknowledged, and we can suppose that the details remaining vague to him pertained less to Hyacinth's love of beauty—a subject on which James already felt more deeply than perhaps anyone then alive—than to Hyacinth's social faith as a worthy alternative to that love. Here he would be breaking new personal ground.[5] And here it can be useful to follow him initially in his letters written while the novel was in process.

In these 1885–86 letters to his brother William, Grace Norton, and Charles Eliot Norton, James comments regularly on contemporary public affairs, which included a sex scandal involving a leading politician, a bomb set off in London by "Irish dynamiters,"[6] a military defeat in the Sudan, and a riot by the London unemployed who smashed the windows of houses three doors from James's while he was out of town—or, in other words, multiple episodes of proletarian protest and colonial resistance to the British capitalism that socialism was attempting to challenge.

Some of James's reaction to all this is standard hostility and denial: he says, for example, that no matter how the Home Rule debate turns out, the Irish will have a civil war in which "they will stew, in a lively enough manner, in their own juice" (3:122–3); and, in a classic reflex of hegemonic self-deception, he says that the London riot was the work not of the "real unemployed" but of "the great army of roughs and thieves" (3:115).[7]

All the more remarkable, then, amidst such statements are James's repeated reflections on the decline of England as a historical process transpiring before his fascinated eyes. To Charles Eliot Norton he compares the "rotten and *collapsible*" condition of the British upper classes to that of the French aristocracy before the Revolution, or, even better, "the heavy, congested, and depraved Roman world upon which the barbarians came down." But this time, he says, the barbarians will come up—"from the black depths of the (in the people) enormous misery" (3:146). After telling William that the London riots were the work of roughs and thieves, he goes on to say that "there is, at any rate, immense destitution. Every one here is growing poorer—from causes which, I fear, will continue" (3:115). And to Grace Norton he writes,

> The possible *malheurs*, reverses, dangers, embarrassments, the "decline," in a word, of old England, go to my heart, and I can imagine no spectacle more touching, more thrilling and even dramatic, than to see this great, precarious, artificial empire, on behalf of which, nevertheless, so much of the strongest and finest stuff of the greatest race (for such they are) has been expended, struggling with forces which, perhaps, in the long run will prove too many for it. (3: 64–5)

Thus overlapping his political temporizing is his vocational excitement at being a witness to history. He had insisted in "The Art of Fiction" on an analogy between painting and fiction—"as the picture is reality, so the novel is history"[8]—and his sense of England's decline as thrilling and dramatic reflects an aroused historical imagination markedly misaligned with his personal politics. This may also explain his notebook entry that the subject of *The Princess* is "magnificent" but that he has never been less clear about how to proceed. For if he sees no end to the "immense destitution" produced by Britain's "artificial Empire," then the socialism he incorporates in his "magnificent subject" asks to be dignified not only rhetorically, as a believable tragic alternative for his hero, but also historically, as capitalism's self-created antagonist. This combined pressure of socialism is enough to threaten James's personal politics, and in giving his mind generously to his novel so that its form would shape itself, he was impelled to plunge headlong into compositional difficulties that he could not be confident in advance of resolving.

2

The form that finally shaped itself was a *Bildungsroman* in which Hyacinth Robinson, a bastard child raised in poverty and apprenticed to a bookbinder, develops both the aesthetic sensibility of a skilled artisan and the proletarian sympathy of a wage-laborer. After becoming an anarchist and swearing before the great leader Hoffendahl to perform an assassination when called upon, he is introduced to the world of art and literature on a scale he could not have imagined by the Princess Casamassima, a breathtaking aristocrat sympathetic to anarchism. His deepening conflict as he awaits his signal is then mainly represented through his relations with the Princess and with Millicent Henning, his childhood playmate of the London slums. By the time his signal comes to assassinate the Duke, both women have betrayed him sexually, leaving him only his beloved London as a source of solace and guidance. London exists for him by now as both "an immeasurable breathing monster" and "the richest expression in the life of man" (2:266); and as if under its aegis, he turns his gun on himself.

James's representation of the European civilization to which Hyacinth is introduced by the Princess is effortless and compelling. That is, after all, the civilization for which he had become an expatriate and also developed his "international novel," whose American characters are challenged to enlarge themselves by mastering the complexity of European manners, morals, and the art they produced. Hyacinth is like those Americans, and *The Princess* is like James's international novels in representing European ripeness by physical description of houses and landscapes. When Hyacinth visits the Princess at her rented country house,

> One of the gardens . . . took the young man's heart beyond the others; it had high brick walls, on the sunny sides of which was a great training of apricots and plums; it had straight walks bordered with old-fashioned homely flowers and enclosing immense squares where other fruit trees stood upright and mint and lavender floated in the air. In the southern quarter it overhung a small disused canal, and here a high embankment had been raised, which was also long and broad and covered with fine turf . . . at either end was a curious pavilion, in the manner of a tea-house, which crowned the scene in an old-world sense and offered rest and privacy, a refuge from sun and shower . . . One of these pavilions . . . was covered inside with a queer Chinese paper representing ever so many times over a group of people with faces like blind kittens, groups who drank tea while they sat on the floor . . . On a shelf over a sofa which was not very comfortable, though it had cushions of faded tapestry that resembled samplers, stood a row of novels out of date and out of print—novels that one couldn't have found any more and that were only there. (2:20)

Here severely excerpted in its ravishing prose is what James mostly meant in his biography of Hawthorne by his notorious catalogue of the features of English life missing from America. They have been missing also for Hyacinth Robinson, and not even his later trip to Paris and Venice will affect him like his week at Medley.

The Medley episode is the climax of his exposure, as a "sensitive nature . . . capable of profiting by all the civilization" England represents, to everything his socialism would destroy.[9]

3

Hyacinth's socialism is represented not only by the small-time plotters arguing over their beer in the smoke-filled Sun and Moon, but also by the other major characters—the Princess and Paul Muniment. Although James makes these people's motives suspect in many ways, they are his chosen principals, and he repeatedly recognizes on their behalf the motive for socialism in the exploitation and misery of the working class.[10]

True, he does not represent this misery directly in the manner of Gaskell's *Mary Barton* or Dickens's *Hard Times*, two novels he would have known, or in anything like the detail he lavishes on Hyacinth's sojourn at Medley. That came from firsthand knowledge, and here he is diplomatically more distant and abstract, with frequent references to, but not scenes of, Lady Aurora's work among the poor, and frequent generalizations about London misery emanating from the other characters. Even Madame Grandoni, no friend of socialism, says, "But there are some things—heaven forbid we should forget them! The misery of London's fearful" (2:312).

Yet neither does James elide or evade the evidence of exploitation and misery in the manner of Dostoevsky and Conrad. There is in fact a surprising number of parallels between *The Princess* and Dostoevsky's *Demons*, of which Dostoevsky later wrote that his entire purpose was to show how naive young socialists could become willing followers of the nihilist Sergei Nechaiev, who orchestrated and performed the political murder that became *Demons*'s organizing episode.[11] But Dostoevsky's extensive notebooks for *Demons* reveal a process of gestation in which this sympathetic purpose was eliminated. In the finished novel those attending the political meeting leading to the murder are said to include "the type of the first and noblest impulse of fervent youth."[12] But neither of the two ideologies debated at the meeting can possibly arouse any noble impulse, and the only type of youth who speak at the meeting are the patently ignoble college student and high school student. Meanwhile, *Demons*'s Shpigulin factory workers are no more than a place-marker for socialism: their exploitation is mentioned only once, and then by the cynical Nechaiev figure Pyotr Verkhovensky, so that its actual significance is rhetorically masked. Dostoevsky's later statement of purpose notwithstanding, *Demons* effectively denies the motive for socialism.

James's narrator, by contrast, in anticipating a workers' meeting at the Sun and Moon during a very hard winter, says in his own voice that "as in that lower world one walked with one's ear nearer the ground the deep perpetual groan of London misery seemed to swell and swell and form the whole undertone of life." Then at the meeting we hear "that in the east of London that night there were forty thousand men out of work" (1:343–4) before this "*exalted deluded* company" proceed to their "blundering divided counsels" (1:358; my emphasis).

And in at least two places James is sharply specific. One is Rosy Muniment's telling Hyacinth how her father became a coal miner at age ten and how

> He never had a day's schooling in his life, but he climbed up out of his black hole into daylight and air, and he invented a machine . . . for use in machine-shops, a mechanical improvement—a new kind of beam-fixing, whatever that is—and he sold it at Bradford for fifteen pounds: I mean the whole right and profit of it and every hope and comfort of his family. (1:141–2)

The other is Hyacinth's image of what his orphan's life would have been if he had not been adopted: "The workhouse and the gutter, ignorance and cold, filth and tatters . . . vermin, starvation and blows . . ." (2:110).[13]

Such passages are few, but they seem to me sufficient to ground in realist documentation the socialist aspirations of the major characters, and most especially to put Hyacinth's conflict on the way to becoming genuinely tragic. They manifest in the novel's form a proletarian shadow world that keeps Hyacinth's susceptibility to beauty from engulfing him entirely. But then as the novel fissures, James transposes Hyacinth's conflict between art and revolution into his personal relations with the Princess and Millicent, both of whom betray him, and in that misogynist diversion he degrades both the Princess's socialism and Millicent's plebeianism. This oblique "safety-valve" attack on socialism through the women characters threatens to subvert Hyacinth's socialist tragedy in progress among the men. But then after the women's betrayals, James restores Hyacinth to London, "the great city which was most his own" (2:266), where his now deepened tragedy can be recovered and consummated.

4

Madame Grandoni speaks for all the characters in describing the Princess's appearance: "She always looks the same: like an angel who came down from heaven yesterday and has been rather disappointed by her first day on earth" (1:272). This icon of Atlantic civilization is also an aspiring socialist, and thus a potential compatriot to Hyacinth on both sides of his divided loyalty. But then

James gives her socialism deeply contradictory motives. On the one hand, he gives evidence for her view of "the imbecility of the people who all over Europe had the upper hand" (1:293) by his depictions of her husband—"as ignorant as one of the dingy London sheep browsing before them, and as contracted as his hat-band" (1:304)—and of the aristocrat Lady Marchant visiting Medley with her daughters, one of whom "had a handsome inanimate face, over which the firelight played without making it more lively, a beautiful voice and the occasional command of a few short words" (2:29).

But then James also depicts the Princess—emphatically but not consistently—as a socialist dilettante motivated only by boredom and caprice. Madame Grandoni says, "she must try everything; at present she's . . . going all lengths in radicalism" (1:305) and later calls her a "*capricciosa*"(2:150). Hyacinth also frequently questions her motives and reflects near the end that "To ask himself if she were in earnest was now an old story to him, and indeed the conviction he might arrive at on this head had ceased to have any high importance" (2:259–60).

Yet James also produces telling evidence against the Princess as *capricciosa*. At Medley she tells Hyacinth that she too had an interview with Hoffendahl but that "he doesn't trust women" (2:51) and in London declined to meet with her. Later, back in London, she works among the poor and becomes deeply involved in the revolutionary underground. Still later, when she sees Hyacinth losing faith in the cause but still feeling bound by his oath, she asks Muniment to arrange for her to replace Hyacinth as designated assassin, and Muniment looks at the floor and says, "I don't trust women—I don't trust clever women!" (2:231).

Perhaps it is possible to attribute even all this to boredom and caprice. But that would also require us to see the Princess as exceptionally talented and exceptionally driven—almost even finely aware and richly responsible. As a once-provincial American capable of all the refinement we now see in her, she sold herself conventionally in marriage, and although her husband turned out to be "the greatest bore in Europe" (1:291), she left him only when he accused her falsely of lying, and now her socialist desire is thwarted by men who don't trust women.

This image of the Princess, whose complex history and motivation might then make her a sympathetic co-protagonist with Hyacinth, also might explain James's naming the novel for her, which hardly seems warranted for a mere *capricciosa*.[14] But James doesn't sustain this image either, and he is finally impelled to impart his rhetorical stress to the Princess, *viz.*:

1 In asking Muniment to take her as Hyacinth's substitute, she says, "I love him [Hyacinth] very much," *and the narrator adds*, "it would have been impossi-

ble for the most impudent cynic to smile at the manner in which she made the declaration" (2:227).

2 Yet when Mr. Vetch, who also loves Hyacinth, comes to plead with her to "get the boy out of his muddle" (2:244), she incomprehensibly stonewalls until Vetch proposes to go directly to Muniment.

3 She then offers to intercede with Muniment, out of a desire "to protect Paul Muniment from the imputation that was in Mr. Vetch's mind" (2:252)—that is, to protect the man who doesn't trust women from the same imputation that was in her mind when she had already failed to move him on Hyacinth's behalf.

4 She then tells Muniment that shielding him from Vetch was part of her plan to secure his help in getting Hyacinth "out of his scrape" (2:298)—that is, her plan to spin her wheels and try promptly again what she had failed in before.

There is more, but I hope this already shows James's narrative fraying in response to the pressure of his need to degrade the Princess's socialism. Unwilling to make her as consistent a socialist as she is a pianist, he transmutes her political drama into sexual melodrama. When there is no longer any reason to attend the clandestine meeting where she now has no hope of extricating Hyacinth, she and Muniment go anyway, simply so they can be seen coming home by Hyacinth and the Prince hiding in the street at 11 P.M., at which scandalous hour Muniment accompanies the Princess into her house. She has been made finally to abandon a man she loves beyond any cynic's impudent smile so that she can thrill to a man who doesn't trust women.

5

Millicent Henning, Hyacinth's childhood playmate who worked her way out of their slum, "was to her blunt, expanded finger-tips a daughter of London . . . it had entered into her blood and her bone, the sound of her voice and the carriage of her head; she understood it by instinct and loved it with passion" (1:60). And this daughter of London

> had no theories about redeeming or uplifting the people; she simply loathed them, for being so dirty, with the outspoken violence of one who had known poverty and the strange bedfellows it makes . . . But for our hero she . . . summed up the sociable humorous ignorant chatter of the masses, their capacity for offensive and defensive passion, their instinctive perception of their strength on the day they should really exercise it. (1:163–4)

For all that Hyacinth is uplifted during the novel by the art, literature, and history represented by the Princess, Medley, and Paris, he also recognizes that Millicent's "mingled beauty and grossness, her vulgar vitality, the spirit of contradiction yet at the same time attachment that was in her, had ended by making her indispensable to him" (2:66).

In the chapter following Muniment's nighttime entrance to the Princess's house, a desolate Hyacinth proposes to Millicent a Sunday outing, and James's account of their London day matches in style and feeling the Medley chapters involving the Princess. As they walk in the park after some customary mutual chaffing, Hyacinth opens himself to Millicent as he has never done before. He tells her of his parentage and confirms her guess that the Princess has dropped him for Muniment. Millicent is newly affectionate to him and eloquent with outrage for his whole life's adversity, and they finally come round to telling each other that their talk has made them seem nicer to each other. Then the chapter ends with the novel's only kiss.

But James no more rests with this image of Millicent than his first image of the Princess. Hyacinth in his last extremity, having received his summons and decided the Princess is lost to him, goes out to walk "in the great indifferent city he so knew and so loved . . . and London had never appeared to him to wear more proudly and publicly the stamp of her imperial history" (2:419–20). This image of London swiftly merges into an image of Millicent:

> All he had ever liked in her came back to him now with a finer air, and there was a moment when he asked himself if at bottom he hadn't liked her better almost than anyone. . . . Something of that sort had really passed between them on Sunday. (2: 420–21)

But when he now goes to look for her at the store where she models clothes, he finds her modeling her body before the lascivious Captain Sholto. Here James drives a last nail into his diversionary denouement and leaves Hyacinth alone in his beloved city resolved to shoot himself.

6

James has meanwhile produced a parallel denouement that itself leads Hyacinth to suicide and makes the women's betrayals superfluous. Beyond and behind the Princess and Millicent, Hyacinth has had all along a transcendent love for London in all the contradiction of its imperial history. His final impulse toward Millicent is inseparable from his love of London, and through all his oscillations between radical politics and civilized refinement, his travels to the country and the Continent, London has remained his necessary element.

The London in whose East End are forty thousand men out of work is also the London in whose Hyde Park "he wanted to drive in every carriage, to mount on every horse, to feel on his arm the hand of every pretty woman in the place" (1:-169–70). And after Medley and Paris and Venice have enlarged and deepened his first response to Hyde Park, he returns to London as if to his first and best lover:

> As the great city which was most his own lay round him under her pall like an immeasurable breathing monster he felt with a vague excitement . . . that it was the richest expression in the life of man. There were nights when everyone he met appeared to reek with gin and filth and . . . he wondered what fate there could be in the great scheme of things for a planet overgrown with such vermin. . . . If it was the fault of the rich . . . that made no difference and only shifted the shame; since the terrestrial globe, a visible failure, produced the cause as well as the effects. (2: 266–68)

London's conjunction of proud imperial history with people reeking with filth constitutes its richness, and socialism's aroused opposition to this richness makes the terrestrial globe seem a visible failure.[15] Hyacinth's awareness here is tragic, and it sustains his commitment to the revolutionary cause despite his devastating reservations:

> What was most in Hyacinth's mind was the idea . . . that the flood of democracy was rising over the world . . . that whatever it might fail to bring, it would at least carry in its bosom a magnificent energy. . . . When this high healing uplifting tide should cover the world and float in the new era, it would be its own fault . . . if want and suffering and crime should continue to be ingredients of the human lot. (2: 262–3)

He does not wish simply to immolate himself in the revolution. Just as the narrator first called the revolutionists "exalted" in the same breath as "deluded," here he calls their cause "healing" and "uplifting" in a voice that is not only Hyacinth's. His conclusion that the revolution will have only itself to blame if it cannot redeem people reeking of filth does not reflect an abstract desire for immolation but a concrete historical judgment. The revolution's energy is an historicized energy for which it can be held accountable, and it is for the sake of this accountability that Hyacinth resists the efforts of all who love him to get him out of his oath. Here James's imagination reaches to socialism's anxiety for itself, and if Hyacinth is self-deluded, it is not in the political naiveté with which he is often charged but in the error of judgment made by someone finely aware and richly responsible that led James to compare him with Hamlet and Lear.

7

The force of imagination that led James to connect bourgeois society's dominant anxiety with revolutionary socialism's emergent anxiety also led him toward Marx and Engels's tragic view of history as a contradictory process. Jeffrey Vogel argues that Marx and Engels saw the Enlightenment values of human rights and human progress as subject to an "irreconcilable conflict" that is "unavoidably painful."[16] Whereas liberal thinkers like John Stuart Mill and John Rawls claim it should always be possible to choose an alternative that can be justified in theory to those victimized by one's choice, for Marx and Engels there could be no way to justify to their victims such things as Greek slavery or North American genocide that were nevertheless instrumental to human progress:[17]

> Marx and Engels argue . . . that, during long periods of history, the opportunity for cultural and material progress and innovation by a few has depended on the extorted labor of the many. (41–42)

Marx's lifelong admiration for classical Greece entailed an awareness that without slavery there could have been "no Plato, no Praxiteles, and no Parthenon" (39), and this parallels Hyacinth's awareness of London as both an "immeasurable breathing monster" and "the richest expression in the life of man."

Marx and Engels also recognized that the contemporary bourgeoisie were personally innocent of the evils of capitalism even if their class demise would end the tragic conflict between human rights and human progress. Yet for them revolution becomes at particular junctures a moral responsibility:

> Marx clearly did side with the Paris Commune . . . even though he thought . . . that this first exemplary attempt at working-class democracy would fail. . . . He rarely hesitates to say that certain protests against exploitation by the working class and its political leaders are premature or utopian. (57)

Henry James's historical imagination does not reach to the question whether his revolutionists might be premature. What's crucial for him is the depth at which they are implicated in something as dramatic and thrilling as England's decline, and in Hyacinth Robinson's "healing uplifting tide" threatening to overwhelm a high civilization that also produces untold misery, James's rhetorically actualized honor done to socialism brings him to Marx and Engels's tragic sense of history.

8

The honor done socialism by James's tragedy is then what the New York intellectuals were moved to ignore. Here we jump from the publication of *The Princess* in 1886 to the essays on the novel by Lionel Trilling in 1948 and Irving Howe in 1957—an interval during which the socialist desire aroused by the Russian Revolution was balked by the Revolution's perversion in the Soviet Union and by the ideological narrowness and sporadic duplicity of the CPUSA in New York. The story of New York intellectuals whose formative years in the 1920s and 30s were spent in conflict between socialist desire and party ideology is told in detail by Alan Wald.[18] While it is not the same story for any two individuals, it does have a common outline. As these people witnessed the Revolution's descent into Stalinism and the New York party's tactical zigzags, many polemicized for years on behalf of various non-Stalinist socialisms, and then in the Cold War gave up on socialism entirely and adopted any number of political positions from liberal to reactionary.

Yet also inseparable from CP ideology was Marxism's conception of class as central to human history, and in New York as elsewhere this conception kept many upstanding intellectuals still in the party's orbit, whether as members or not, irrespective of its positions on Stalin or the strategy of the United Front.[19] And just as some anti-Stalinists stayed in or near the party because of its commitment to class, many who opposed the party, including many still avowed socialists, came to ignore class as a specific historical process.

Lionel Trilling and Irving Howe were in several respects at opposite ends of the New York spectrum. Trilling was apparently a brief fellow traveler of the party,[20] whereas Howe remained an independent socialist all his life, founding *Dissent* in the McCarthyite 1950s with the aim of keeping socialist ideas alive in a hostile environment and at age 65 writing *Socialism and America*, where he tried to account for socialism's failure ever to take hold in the United States.

But Trilling no less than Howe remained committed to the connection between politics and literature and felt impelled like Howe to distance his literary criticism from that associated with the party. Anti-Stalinism was their common ground, and it finally led both to dissociate themselves not only from party ideology but also from the historicism of class bound up with that ideology—the historicism James shared in *The Princess* with Marx and Engels.

It was in fact Trilling who rescued *The Princess* from the library-shelf limbo of James's New York Edition, and his 1948 Introduction to the Macmillan reprint then became part of *The Liberal Imagination*. But Trilling's liberal sensibility could not extend James's "imagination of love," as Trilling wonderfully called it, to an embrace of his hero's socialism specifically in its class motivation.

Trilling cites James's letters to William and the Nortons partly to the same effect I do, and he characterizes the novel's tragedy in terms close to mine:

> A vulgar and facile progressivism can find this [Hyacinth's suicide] to be a proof of James's "impotence in matters sociological"—"the problem remains unsolved." Yet it would seem that a true knowledge of society . . . knows that sometimes society offers an opposition of motives in which the antagonists are in such a balance of authority and appeal that a man who so fully perceives them as to embody them in his very being cannot choose between them and is therefore destroyed. This is known as tragedy.[21]

Here he would seem to honor Hyacinth's socialism, in its balance of authority with civilization, just as I have argued James does. But tragedy is not all of one kind, and by ensconcing "society" above "the history of hitherto existing society," and then in making society the source of both our knowledge and Hyacinth's motives, Trilling excludes the possibility that society itself can be tragically subject to historical scrutiny or progressivist change. His de-historicized conception allows for a tragedy like *Othello*, whose conflict is between the values indigenous to a particular society, but not a tragedy like *King Lear*, whose conflict is between the class-bound values of residual and emergent societies.

Trilling then goes on to elaborate an exclusively psychological analysis of Hyacinth's tragedy:

> By the time Hyacinth's story draws to its end, his mind is in a perfect equilibrium, not of irresolution but of awareness . . . And just as he is in an equilibrium of awareness, he is also in an equilibrium of guilt . . . There is for him as little doubt of the revolution's success as there is of the fact that his mother had murdered his father. And when he thinks of revolution, it is as a tremendous tide, a colossal force; he is tempted to surrender to it as an escape from his isolation . . . But if the revolutionary passion *thus* has its guilt, Hyacinth's passion for life at its richest and noblest is no less guilty . . . One cannot "accept" the suffering of others, no matter if one's own suffering be also accepted, without incurring guilt. It is the guilt in which every civilization is implicated. (85–6; my emphasis)

Here he translates Hyacinth's contingent politics into universal psychology. He says the revolutionary's guilt is that of relieving one's isolation by immolating one's self in a cause whose success one is sure of in advance.[22] But when Hyacinth reflects that it will be the revolution's own fault "if want and suffering and crime should continue," he is neither isolated as yet nor certain in advance of the revolution's success. He is acknowledging it might fail and is thereby accepting, not the abstract guilt of immolation but the concrete contingency of his emancipatory desire.

Similarly, Trilling's claim that one cannot accept others' suffering without incurring a guilt in which every civilization is implicated entails the Mill–Rawls liberal argument as Jeffrey Vogel describes it. It assumes that civilization is built necessarily on human suffering, and it then has no way to explain that suffering except by human perfidy. Thus where I have claimed for James a not-so-facile historical tragedy implicating the doctrine of Progress, Trilling is backed into claiming a psychological tragedy implicating the doctrine of Original Sin.

9

Irving Howe's socialism was a Platonic socialism that defined itself ethically in response to existing socialisms rather than historically in response to the dynamics of class. Howe, like Trilling, is impelled to ignore James's homage to socialism in his chapter on *The Princess* in *Politics and the Novel*. He too has a passage under which I could almost enlist my reading of *The Princess*:

> The book registered his [James's] fear that everything he valued was crumbling . . . but it also betrayed his doubt whether, in some ultimate moral reckoning that was beyond his grasp, everything did not deserve to crumble. This could hardly affect his conservative temper . . . but it did permit him a breadth of feeling greater than is usually available to those in whom conservatism is merely an opinion.[23]

But here I would need to turn some of Howe's words against him and say that James's unusual breadth of feeling put exactly within his grasp the ultimate reckoning that everything he valued deserved to crumble. In *The Princess* it enabled his conservative temper to transcend his conservative opinion and thrill to the spectacle of England's class-bound decline—and then also, at a crucial juncture, to make Hyacinth's socialism prospectively accountable for failures that were to become all too familiar to Howe's generation in retrospect.

Howe's commitment to socialism, that is, gave him every reason to recognize and welcome James's representation of both capitalism's and socialism's anxiety for themselves as part of a single, contradictory process. But he was disarmed from doing that by having omitted class from his socialist commitment—Howe once said that what he and his cofounders of *Dissent* "meant by socialism" was no more than "some vision of the good—or at least a better—society."[24] This highly idealized and diluted socialism is finally indistinguishable from Trilling's liberalism, and where Trilling dehistoricizes *The Princess* by oversimplifying its tragedy, Howe dehistoricizes it by ignoring its tragedy and apparently wishing for another kind of novel. In one passage he characterizes Hyacinth Robinson all but unknowingly in tragic terms reminiscent of Trilling's:

> And it is here that Hyacinth becomes an almost archetypal figure. Torn between the claims of the future and the claims of the past, between a vision of human fraternity in a world not yet made and the tangible glories of the cultural edifice, he is now, for the first time and at a fearful cost, fully sensitive to the possibilities of life. (155)

But this "first time" (Hyacinth's afternoon with Paul Muniment in Chapter XXXV, three-fourths through the novel) is not for Howe part of a tragic progression. It is a discontinuous chapter—"probably the best in the book" (154)—in a novel that he has also said lacks a unified plot and remains "a bewildering mixture of excellence and badness" (141). Howe identifies Hyacinth's place in this mixture by saying that James lacked "some motivating idea about the revolutionary movement . . . [which] was indispensable for bringing into full play the energies that lay waiting in the novel" (150) and that this deficiency

> might have been overcome . . . if James had chosen as his hero a figure of strength who would impose himself on the political environment. . . . Hyacinth Robinson, however, is one of the most passive of James's heroes. He is a youth, James writes, "on whom nothing is lost," and that is true. . . . But he is also a youth on whom nothing rubs off. (152)

That makes Hyacinth sound a little like Hamlet, which would surely have pleased James, but then Howe also writes of Hyacinth's "languorous passivity" and "snobbism" (152), his "fatal flaw of acquired gentility" that leaves him "unable to act on his desires" (153), and his "moral smugness"(154)—which makes him sound more like one of Dickens's or Eliot's febrile aristocrats. Hyacinth's passivity cannot overcome the novel's lack of a motivating idea, and thus Howe's need for a different kind of hero. But his suggested hero—strong enough to impose himself on the political environment—also sounds incapable of any tragic conflict involving either capitalism's or socialism's anxiety for themselves. And without seeing the class process involved in such a conflict, Howe also couldn't see how closely *The Princess* touches on the anxiety for socialism that motivated his own career.

Neither Trilling nor Howe felt threatened by socialism in the abstract but only by its contemporary betrayals. While James represents the possibility of such betrayals only in the passage where Hyacinth reflects that socialism will have but itself to blame if human suffering continues, his entire tragic progression requires and generates that passage. There above all James transcends his conservative opinions in the form itself of his novel, and despite Trilling's awareness of Hyacinth's tragedy and Howe's claim that his critique is not ideological, neither is motivated to an analysis of *The Princess* through which such a passage can register its effect.[25] In finally misapprehending a tragic conflict that encompasses the historic anxieties aroused by socialism, they markedly misrepresent James's proto-Marxian novel finally shaped by the imagination of love.

Trilling's and Howe's analyses also foretell the evacuation of class from subsequent criticism of *The Princess Casamassima*. Perhaps the most widely influential essay after theirs is Mark Seltzer's explication of panoptical surveillance as the novel's informing vision.[26] In Seltzer's Foucauldian perspective James's historicism of class becomes invisible, just as in the scholarship of identity categories class remains all but invisible as a site alongside gender and ethnicity. The perspective in which class may become visible, not as a site but as an identity-forming process continuously entailed by the production and distribution of surplus labor, is necessarily historical and is fundamentally constituted by that nonpareil of master narratives, *The Communist Manifesto*. Henry James, against all odds, was moved to enter that narrative, and in the repressed polemic against history entailed by their overt polemic against Stalinism, his New York critics effectively repositioned him for a new generation.

5
THE GRAMSCIAN ORDEAL OF MERIDEL LE SUEUR

> One must speak of a struggle for a new culture, that is, for a new moral life . . . until it becomes a new way of feeling and seeing reality and, therefore, a world intimately ingrained in "possible artists" and "possible works of art." —ANTONIO GRAMSCI

> I did not know how to make, enlarge, and limn the image of solidarity. I did not know what the action of transformation was. —MERIDEL LE SUEUR

Meridel Le Sueur's erratic career as a writer of fiction both illustrates and challenges Gramsci's theory of organic intellectuals as those produced by any class in the process of its formation. Le Sueur was born in 1900, nine years after Gramsci; she joined the American Communist Party in 1924, the year he became secretary-general of the Italian Socialist Party; she published her first story in 1927, a year after he was imprisoned; and in 1935, the year ill health brought to an end the writing collected in his *Prison Notebook*, she articulated a conception of organic intellectual all but identical to that of his *Prison Notebooks*. Le Sueur then struggled in her writing for another sixty years to become that organic intellectual, and her defeat in that struggle exemplifies the tragic experience often required but never quite acknowledged by Gramsci's theory.

Gramsci regards organic intellectuals as indispensable to the process by which his famous "hegemony" is formed and nurtured. He defines hegemony as "the 'spontaneous' consent given by the great masses of the population to the general direction imposed on social life by the dominant fundamental group"[1]—a code phrase for the ruling class—and he goes on to claim that the hegemony of any class is largely created by its organic intellectuals—those produced directly by that class and who give it "homogeneity and an awareness of its own function not only in the economic but also in the social and political fields" (5).

Gramsci had witnessed two great defeats of the left before his imprisonment—of the workers' factory councils that successfully operated the Turin auto plants in 1919–20 and then of the Socialist and Communist parties striving to block Mussolini's accession to power. His theory of hegemony, as it then took shape in the *Prison Notebooks*, can be viewed in part as a response to those defeats by requiring a period of gestation in which an emergent class develops a nascent counter-hegemony, through a cultural "war of position" within civil society, before trying to contend for power through a strategic "war of maneuver" in the politics of the national state.

Organic intellectuals are necessary to create this counter-hegemony, and, while they often emerge directly from the new class, they are also regularly recruited from among "traditional intellectuals"—politically uncommitted professionals produced by an accelerating division of labor: engineers and city planners, lawyers and accountants, teachers, scholars, and artists—whose skills help create and sustain the social infrastructure required by any hegemonic group. These are also very often the heirs of formerly organic intellectuals whose hegemonic groups have been historically superseded—for example, Catholic clergy once organic to feudal aristocracy who then become available for conversion to monarchical absolutism, capitalist imperialism, or liberation theology. To become organic intellectuals, they must become partisans of a new hegemony through "active participation in practical life, as constructor, organiser, 'permanent persuader' and not just a simple orator" (10). They do this primarily by means of the political party, which keeps them in touch with the masses and which is also "responsible for welding together the organic intellectuals of a given group . . . and the traditional intellectuals" (15).[2] The party is not a Leninist vanguard that will establish the relationship between intellectuals and the masses after the revolution has occurred but a seedbed in which that relationship is cultivated beforehand in order for the revolution to succeed.

As a member of the Communist Party, Le Sueur struggled to reconstitute her modernist (i.e., "traditional") intellectual's devotion to the Demeter myth and D. H. Lawrence, both of which, she told interviewers, "saved my life" when she was young,[3] from her traditionally symbolic representations to newly realistic representations that would embody the emergent *processes* of a feminist–proletarian hegemony. This struggle transpires in a variety of short fiction and journalism published during the 1920s and 30s, and it culminates in two ideologically incommensurate novellas both finished at the end of the 1930s—*The*

Girl and *I Hear Men Talking*. By that time the CP's Popular Front strategy was about to weaken its capacity for counter-hegemony, Le Sueur was about to be silenced by McCarthyism, and any possibility of transcending the conflict embodied by the two novellas, between a "traditional" modernism and an "organic" new realism, was for the moment foreclosed. Then when Le Sueur came to write again in the 1970s and 80s, after being rediscovered by a new generation of feminists and radicals, she reverted to her earlier modernist representation, which was also second nature to her new audience in its innocence of political institutions wherein women and workers might incubate collectively an alternative hegemony and its mode of representation.

Although Gramsci noted the difficulty involved for traditional intellectuals in becoming organic intellectuals, he seems not to have anticipated such possibilities as the political party's disappearance as a medium of transformation. Le Sueur arrived independently at something like Gramsci's theory for avoiding new defeats. Even so, she was defeated, as he had been, as if the historical process he theorized were more chaotic, overdetermined, and potentially tragic than he could yet acknowledge in the *Prison Notebooks*.

1

Le Sueur's North American matrilineal heritage made her a prime candidate for conversion to organic proletarian intellectual. Her great-grandmother was an Iroquois, and her gunslinging grandmother helped settle Oklahoma while divorcing her husband for drinking up the farm, sang "Jesus, Lover of My Soul, Let Me to Thy Bosom Fly" when bathing under her shift, and in parades of the Women's Christian Temperance Union dressed her granddaughter all in white to sing "Lips that touch liquor shall never touch mine!" She helped put her daughter through college, and when this daughter, Marian Wharton (1877–1950), later kidnapped her children—Meridel and two brothers—from another alcoholic husband, she became a socialist and a Chatauqua lecturer on women's rights.

During Le Sueur's formative years, according to Howard Zinn,

> The strongest Socialist state organization was in Oklahoma, which in 1914 had twelve thousand dues-paying members (more than New York State), and elected over a hundred Socialists to local office, including six to the Oklahoma legislature. There were fifty-five weekly Socialist newspapers in Oklahoma, Texas, Louisiana, and Arkansas, and summer encampments that drew thousands of people.[4]

Le Sueur recalled for her part how

> In Oklahoma they had the moonlight schools where, after harvest, the whole family camped out. There were classes in economics, socialism, history, and there was dancing to the fiddle and accordian [sic], and home theater with skits and poetry and original song and home-grown comics. And the children had special education in mutual aid that taught them how it was better to lift a rock together . . . It was a counter-culture of collectivity instead of dog-eat-dog. [5]

Le Sueur's stepfather, Arthur Le Sueur (1867–1950), was descended from French refugees of 1848, grew up in Minnesota, graduated from the University of Michigan Law School in 1891, and was Socialist mayor of Minot, North Dakota (1912–16), before becoming President of the People's College in Fort Scott, Kansas, a workers' correspondence school whose chancellor was Eugene Debs and whose English department head was now Marian Wharton.

Arthur and Marian married in 1917, and Le Sueur later wrote that "It was in Fort Scott that I got my education" (*C*, xxi). The trustees of the People's College included Helen Keller and Charles Steinmetz, and its visitors included Alexander Berkman and the starving survivors of the 1914 "Ludlow Massacre" in Colorado—blacklisted miners who during their failed strike were evicted from their company homes and then saw their tents set afire by the National Guard, which also killed thirteen people while two mothers and thirteen children were burning to death beneath the tents. Le Sueur recalled walking with those miners down the streets of Fort Scott—she would have been sixteen—as "one of the great experiences of my life, changing me forever" (*C*, xvii), and her last published work, *The Dread Road*, when she was 90, is full of allusions to Ludlow.

The midwest Socialist party's opposition to World War I led to the destruction by vigilantes of the People's College. The Le Sueurs moved to St. Paul, where their new home became a cross-country stop for union organizers and radicals. Le Sueur remembered among others Joe Hill and Big Bill Haywood, Woody Guthrie and Pete Seeger, Lincoln Steffens and Ella (Mother) Bloor, and of course Eugene Debs. Her youth was thus steeped in midwestern radicalism, and after she left home she connected as a matter of course with the bi-coastal urban radicalism of the Socialist and Communist parties. In New York, where she went first to study acting, she lived with Emma Goldman and Alexander Berkman in their commune, and after then moving to Hollywood in 1922, she got a few bit parts, worked as a stunt girl, refused to submit her "Semitic" nose to cosmetic surgery, and was dropped from the radio part of Betty Crocker because her voice was too sexy for the kitchen.[6]

She then worked in California restaurants, factories, and little theaters, joining the Communist Party in 1924 and publishing her first story in 1927. By then she was writing regularly for *The Daily Worker*, and throughout the thirties she published journalism and fiction in both mainstream and radical journals: *American Mercury*, *Dial*, *Scribner's*, and *Yale Review*; *The Anvil*, *New Masses*, and *Partisan Review*. She was also at various times on the staff of *New Masses*, a member of the Workers Alliance and the John Reed Club, a worker in the Federal Writers Project, and a participant in the 1934 Twin Cities Teamsters strike. In 1940 twelve of her stories were collected in *Salute to Spring*, and in 1945 *North Star Country*, her mythic history of the Midwest, became a Book Find Club selection. What reputation she had rested on those two books until John Crawford and Elaine Hedges began reprinting her other work in the 1970s and 80s (Coiner, 80–82).[7]

Le Sueur told Elaine Hedges that she began writing her first story at a time when she felt

> rejected by her own mother and "lost" in the male-controlled world of Hollywood. "I wanted and expected to kill myself. . . . I was already dead," she recalls, and she did attempt suicide at the time. Writing the story, with its controlling myth of Demeter and Persephone, sustained her. (Hedges, 4)

Yet her continuing struggle for sustenance did not lead her to reject either the radical culture in which she grew up or that of the CP. In her writing she proceeded to make her Demeter and Persephone figures renew fertility in the scorched lives of farm and working women, and in her career as a writer after leaving the male-controlled world of Hollywood, she regularly challenged the male-controlled world of the party. In a 1938 journal entry she wrote, "It isn't any wonder people feel religious about the party. It is love, wife, children to us" (Coiner, 95). To both Elaine Hedges and Constance Coiner she called the party "nourishing" (Hedges, 8; Coiner, 91).[8] And in a 1995 interview, when asked whether she was still a party member, the bedridden 95-year-old replied, "Prone, but still in!"[9] Socialism was for Le Sueur what Aijaz Ahmad calls "the emancipatory desire of our epoch," and throughout her life her prairie heritage sustained her artistic struggle on behalf of the party's socialist aspirations.

2

That struggle sometimes put her superficially at odds with party ideologues like Whitaker Chambers, who called her thirties depictions of women's suffering defeatist, or with *New Masses* editors whom she called "doctrinaire" in criticizing her "lyrical style" as "undisciplined" (Coiner, 96; Hedges, 14). But hers was a far deeper struggle to produce a voice of proletarian womanhood, and she herself defined this struggle in her Gramscian polemic on "The Fetish of Being Outside."

Published in *New Masses*, February 26, 1935, "The Fetish . . ." is a reply to the poet Horace Gregory, who had questioned in his *New Masses* essay whether writers shouldn't stay outside the party even when they believed in its vision: since this was a vision of something that doesn't yet exist, it could undermine the writer's engagement with what does exist, free of "the heat of conflict." Le Sueur called Gregory's position a "subtle equivocation"[10] through which he could be inside and outside both at once. But she also recognized in his argument something symptomatic for herself as subject to a "middle class malady" (199) in which she regards her personal experience as "special and precious" (200). But it is precisely through this malady, Le Sueur argues, that the writer can "break the old forms of psychic reaction . . . and create a new nucleus of communal interaction."

This breakthrough can be accomplished by accepting the writer's "peculiar and prophetic function to stand for a belief in something that scarcely exists" (199 passim):

> This is where the "action" of the writer or creative worker of any kind comes in. It is an action of belief, of full belief. There is some kind of extremity and willingness to walk blind that comes in any creation of a new and unseen thing, some kind of final last step that has to be taken *with full intellectual understanding and with the artist, a step beyond that too, a creation of a future "image," a future action that exists in the present even vaguely* . . . only in a raised arm, or a word dropped in the dark but from these, because of full belief, he will produce a movement, even a miraculous form that has not hitherto existed. (202; my emphasis)

Here Le Sueur argues for the conversion of Gramsci's traditional intellectual—Horace Gregory?—into an organic intellectual committed by full belief to a hegemony-in-the-making, where "I can no longer live without communal sensibility" (200).

But Gramsci also argued that the process of creating organic intellectuals is "long, difficult, full of . . . advances and retreats, dispersals and regroupings, in which the loyalty of the masses is often sorely tried." For there is an inevitable "gap" between the masses and the intellectuals, since

> one is going through a . . . primitive historical phase . . . which is still economic-corporate, in which the general "structural" framework is being quantitatively transformed and the appropriate quality-superstructure is in the process of emerging, but is not yet organically formed. (334–5)

Where the masses are necessarily preoccupied with quantitative transformations in the "'structural' framework," the intellectuals are preoccupied with the formation of an "appropriate quality-superstructure," and even within one political party the two can't help but be sometimes out of phase.

Le Sueur is also aware of Gramsci's gap when she says that the writer needs to "walk blind" in trying to create the "new and unseen thing" that is also Gramsci's emerging "quality-superstructure," and then again when she says that the writer must enter "a dark chaotic passional world of another class, the proletariat, which is still perhaps unconscious of itself like a great body sleeping, stirring . . . outside the calculated, expedient world of the bourgeoisie" (202).[11] Here her reference to the proletariat as an unconscious body may sound more like Leninist vanguardism than Gramscian organicism. But to walk blind into another world in the hope of finding something previously unseen is far from Leninist, and the passage as a whole can suggest the struggle involved for a traditional intellectual attempting to transform herself into an organic intellectual.

For Le Sueur as for Gramsci there is a second and enabling gap in conducting that struggle, not only between the intellectuals and the masses but also between the masses and the calculated world of the bourgeoisie in its quantitative transformations. The masses are regularly disaffected by those transformations, and through *this* gap the writer can become capable of entering their passional world in a manner to earn their loyalty.

Gramsci said that the masses feel but do not always know, whereas the intellectuals know but do not always feel:

> The intellectual's error consists in believing that one can know without understanding and even more without feeling and being impassioned . . . in other words that the intellectual can be an intellectual . . . if distinct and separate from the people-nation, that is, without feeling the elementary passions of the people, understanding them and therefore explaining and justifying them in the particular historical situation. (418)

That is also Meridel Le Sueur's answer to Horace Gregory when she says that the writer's "last step that has to be taken with full intellectual understanding" is into the passional world of the proletariat, from which will follow "a step beyond that too, a creation of a future 'image'" that will connect the writer with the masses.[12]

"The Fetish of Being Outside" announces the organic aspiration of a traditional intellectual and translates Le Sueur's personal history into a conceptual framework fully congruent with Gramsci's theory of organic intellectuals forging an alternative hegemony. Her one other extant programmatic statement, "Proletarian Literature and the Middle West," also dates from 1935 and is also deeply Gramscian.[13] Both essays were written during a period when she was also producing a great welter of journalism and fiction. The disparateness of this writing, to which I turn next, reflects those "advances and retreats, dispersals and regroupings" that Gramsci said are necessary to the long, difficult process by which organic intellectuals are formed.

3

During Le Sueur's most prolific period, from the late 1920s through the mid-1940s, the diversity of her writing exhibits a ferment in which her mode of representing the Demeter myth moves from a Lawrentian symbolic lyricism toward a feminist-proletarian realism. She increasingly foregrounds gender, class, and their politics as themes, and in narrative viewpoint and style she keeps narrowing the gap between a traditional narrator's symbolic representation and an organic speaker's discursive narration.

One group of short stories published between 1927 and 1935 involves variations on the Demeter myth keyed to latent, repressed, or blighted sexuality in the manner of Lawrence or Sherwood Anderson. These stories link the possibility of human community to the sensibility of women attuned to the land; their omniscient narrators focus on women characters whose transformative response to the seasons of planting and harvesting is balked; and their figurative descriptions make women's alienation from the land a metaphor for the absence of human community.

Two of these stories mark the range of the others: "Persephone," a symbolic rendering of the Demeter myth by a country-girl narrator who watched it unfold, and "Corn Village," a diffuse rumination on prairie cultural poverty by an omniscient narrator who keeps identifying herself as a professional writer. "Persephone" is marked on the one hand by its lush descriptions of Demeter (whose name in the story is Freda!) in her sowing and reaping—

> When we brought her water she straightened from the earth to loom above us, curving against the sky; a strong odor would come from her, like the odor of earth when it is just turned; her yellow hair would glisten around her face and we thought it grew from her head exactly as the wheat grew from the earth [14]

—and on the other hand by its omission of Persephone's seasonal return from the underworld through a bargain with Zeus that allows Demeter's earth to remain fruitful. Instead, Le Sueur's Persephone, having borne all along "the mark of a perpetual death" (77), is being taken to the city for incarceration in a psychiatric hospital, leaving Freda "an old woman whose time of fertility had gone" (81).[15]

The fate of fertility is also the theme of "Corn Village," a discourse on "the emptiness and ghostliness of mid-America,"[16] where man has "no community to give him life. . . . No fund of instinct and experience has been accumulated" (10). The narrator calls this a "mystery" and confesses herself "baffled to know the meaning of people in the Midwest towns" (16). She says Sinclair Lewis got that meaning wrong and Sherwood Anderson got only part of it, for "the whole communal organism suffered perhaps" (17). Finally she says the Midwest's only communal influence is violence and describes her townspeople's responses to a cyclone, a murder/suicide, and a revival, all of which connect people in talk:

> they no longer straggle, stand unwoven, apart, they stand close together, welded together in the lines of their bodies, their heads leaning close, for one of their kind has felt something and let it ripen and come to expression. (19)

But this faint tremor of community, whose only substance is its metaphorical rendering, cannot be sustained after the experience of violence fades, and soon "The great mid-continent vacuum swallows everything again" (24)—as if the land by itself were incapable after all of producing human community.

The other stories in this group—"Spring Story," "The Afternoon," "Harvest," "Holiday," "The Miracle," and "Wind"—explore through omniscient narration different facets of the Midwest's struggle for psychic and cultural fertility. But only in "Spring Story" is this possibly achieved, and here the protagonist is an adolescent village girl whose tremulous epiphany barely promises to outlast the Easter Sunday on which it occurs. The other stories delineate the many forms of blight that await its ripening heroine, and none suggests any basis for the "communal organism" that "Corn Village" identifies as the Midwest's great absence. Instead, they register that absence in tales of isolated individuals permeated by the "lyricism" that Le Sueur defended to *New Masses* editors but later said she regretted in her early work influenced by Lawrence and the Demeter myth.[17]

Overlapping this cluster of stories, Le Sueur produced a heterogeneous array of fiction and reportage whose alternations of subject and style show her searching a way out of the narrative terrain of her Kansas life. Between "Women on the Breadlines" in 1932 and *Salute to Spring* in 1940 are stories of middle-class and working-class women in their differing material and cultural privations; of political organizing and strikes; of pregnancy and premature death. In these writings the distinction between fiction and journalism is often blurred, the narrative perspective jumps around, and the metaphoric lyricism gives way to a spare referential prose as Le Sueur tries to articulate the "communal sensibility" that she had said in "The Fetish . . ." she could no longer live without.

Here also are Lawrentian echoes, as in the overpraised "Annunciation" and the finely wrought "The Girl." In several stories where Le Sueur makes labor organizing instead of the land her medium of communal consciousness, she persists in her earlier mode of metaphoric representation. "Tonight Is Part of the Struggle," for example, depicts a quarreling jobless couple who make up by carrying their infant to a mass meeting. When the Communist speaker at the meeting refers to the hunger marches that preceded it, the wife

> looked down on the great black sea of bodies, heads like black wheat growing from the same soil, the same wind. Something seemed to enter her and congeal. I am part, she wanted to say.[18]

This woman's image of workers' heads growing from one soil reflects what Le Sueur must surely have thought preferable, as an image of communal sensibility in which individuals are united in common purpose, to that reflected by an omniscient narrator's image of heads grouped in gossip after a murder, in which individuals are aggregated without being united. But her metaphoric mode gives her no way to register this political difference, and meanwhile the story gives us no reason to think this wife's epiphany can be sustained beyond its flash of metaphor. Something like this also occurs in "Salute to Spring" and "'Farewell My Wife My Child and All My Friends'."

Interspersed among these are stories in which human community is neither scenic nor metaphorical but a discursively represented process. These mostly urban proletarian stories, drawn from personal experience of Twin Cities poverty and unionization, focus on women, often migrants from ruined farms, scrounging for work while bearing their children and going hungry in the Depression. The presiding season is winter, as befits Demeter bereft of Persephone, and while fertility is still represented by the traditional symbol of pregnancy, community is now represented by an organic intellectual's mimesis of discursive relations among women seeking access to food, jobs, and childcare.

These relations begin with the narrative perspective itself—Le Sueur's rhetorical relation to the women whose capacity for community she aspires to represent. Using her own privation to join her voice to those of women unlike her intellectual self, she zigzags among four perspectives in groping for the persona of an urban Demeter renewing fertility by telling these women's winter's tales through a consciousness akin to their own—a Gramscian organicism in the form of her storytelling itself.

The first stage is professional reportage. In "What Happens in a Strike," Le Sueur the traditional journalist methodically describes the 1934 Minneapolis Teamsters Strike: the strikers' organization and activity, the police firing their shotguns, the massive funeral cortege (actually 40,000 people) for the slain striker. The second stage is personal memoir. In "I Was Marching," also a report on the strike published within a month of "What Happens . . . ," Le Sueur describes her participation at strike headquarters, where she feels at first out of place when put to work washing coffee cups:

> Nobody asks my name. I am given a large butcher's apron. I realize I have never before worked anonymously. . . . We have to wash fast and rinse them and set them up quickly for buttermilk and coffee as the line thickens and the men wait. . . . I feel I won't be able to wash tin cups, but when no one pays any attention except to see that there are enough cups I feel better.[19]

Her discomfort is that of a class and cultural alien who must transform herself internally in a manner not required by her reportage in "What Happens . . . ."[20] The narratorial difference is slight but telling, and then in the third stage is enlarged, as in "Women on the Breadlines," whose narrator shares the poverty of those sitting with her at the employment bureau:

> Bernice sits next to me. She is a Polish woman of thirty-five. She has been working in people's kitchens for fifteen years. . . . She is large, her great body in mounds, her face brightly scrubbed. She has a peasant mind and finds it hard even yet to understand the maze of the city. . . . When you speak to her, her face lifts and brightens as if you had spoken through a great darkness, and she talks magically of little things as if the weather were magic, or tells some crazy story of her adventures on the city streets.[21]

Here the objectified subject of the traditional journalist takes on personal presence, and so does the narrator herself:

> I've lived in cities for many months, broke, without help, too timid to get in bread lines. I've known many women to live like this until they simply faint on the street from privations, without saying a word to anyone. A woman will shut herself up in a room until it is taken away from her, and eat a cracker a day and be quiet as a mouse so there are no social statistics concerning her. (142)

We know that Le Sueur was often hungry and broke, but from what we also know it is hard to believe that she was entirely without help or quite so timid. Isn't she also creating here a rhetorical persona, alien to the traditional journalist in both style and substance, that shrinks the gap between her and women who've worked for years in people's kitchens?[22]

The fourth and final stage is first-person narration wherein women like Bernice speak for themselves in voices now informed by Le Sueur's political awareness. She more than once described the writer's function as recording the voice of the people, and in two stories of this period—"They Wanted Little" and "Sequel to Love"—she tries to capture that voice. The narrator of "Sequel to Love" is incarcerated in a mental institution for as long as she refuses to be sterilized:

> I been cryin' for about three weeks. I'd rather stay in this hole with the cracked ones than have that done to me that's a sin and a crime. I can't be sleeping hardly ever any night yet I'd stay right here than have that sin done to me because then I won't be in any pleasure with a man and that's all the pleasure I ever had. Workers ain't supposed to have any pleasure and now they're takin' that away because it ain't supposed to be doin' anybody any good and they're afraid I'll have another baby.[23]

This is a long way from Le Sueur's earlier omniscient lyricism, but not from the theme of fertility that recurs in stories of this period. Most tellingly in this story, the speaker's final sentence connects fertility with both gender and class in a first-person discourse of political awareness that shrinks the gap between the writer and her subject and produces in embryo a feminist worker intellectual.

4

If we can see Le Sueur's earlier stories as the Lawrentian romances of a traditional intellectual, rooted in her Kansas girlhood, and her later stories as the feminist-proletarian realism of an organic intellectual, rooted in her Twin Cities adulthood, then we can also see that by the end of the Depression her emergent form had not yet displaced her residual form with any real authority. She ended the 1930s by completing two short novels, both begun earlier and neither one published for forty years, which develop the two incommensurate versions of her Demeter myth. *I Hear Men Talking* (1940) is a third-person omniscient narrative depicting a village girl's sexual stirrings and friendships with adult "grotesques" that often echoes *Winesburg, Ohio*. Its protagonist Penelope and her mother Mona also echo Persephone and Demeter, only now Mona's sowing and reaping take the form of organizing farmers facing depressed milk prices and foreclosures. Yet the novel reaches its climax not in the farmers' revolt but in their response to a cyclone whose debris injures Penelope. Lying in bed during her recovery, she hears men talking, not of foreclosure but of what they saw of the cyclone. Then, amidst extensive quotation from this talking on the novel's last page, the narrator interjects with:

> Voices fused together, talking of what they had seen and would see, of a tide they knew now carried them and did not separate them doing battle against each other.[24]

Here is a reprise of the "Corn Village" image of heads together talking as a manifestation of communal consciousness. But this image, now timed so as to inspire Penelope's recovery after her exposure to political organizing, is doubly disappointing. It is unsupported by any preparatory narrative, and it is superimposed on a narrative newly capable of supporting an alternative image of communal consciousness produced by political organizing. Thus even at the end of her proletarian decade with its rhetorical struggle, Le Sueur still can't surrender her myth of nature as the source of community that she said had saved her at the outset.

Both formally and thematically, *The Girl* (1939) couldn't be more different from *I Hear Men Talking*. This is the first-person narrative of a nameless waitress who has migrated to the city from a corn village and whose "ripening" transpires among men who beat their women and women who drink and whore. Like the speaker of "Sequel to Love," the Girl is ready for a man, and in getting her man and seeing him killed in a bank robbery after she resisted abortion and insisted on bearing their child, she enlarges by leaps the nascent political awareness evinced by her predecessor. She becomes a politicized Persephone returned from Hades to reunite with her mother in communal consciousness and activism.

After her lover's death she too is consigned by the welfare authorities to a psychiatric hospital and slated for sterilization once her child is born. But she is rescued by Amelia, the Demeter-like midwife *and* leader of the Workers Alliance, who had six children before her husband was killed in a strike after telling her "he'd rather die fighting than . . . live like a mouse."[25] Amelia brings the Girl to bear her child in a women's commune she has established in an abandoned warehouse, and then in quick succession the following things occur:

1 Another waitress, Clara, is brought to the commune to die from shock treatments administered by the welfare authorities.

2 While the Girl in early labor attends the dying Clara, Amelia leads a demonstration outside the welfare office, which a woman demonstrator later describes to the Girl:

> Kid you should have seen the demonstration, hundreds outside the courthouse and the cops

> threw tear gas out the windows and some of those ballplayers caught the bombs and threw them right back and kid, you should have seen those bureaucrats, like rats, pouring out of the building, and the streets littered with those leaflets saying Milk and Iron Pills for Clara. (145)

3 Clara dies, and the assembling of women to mourn her leads the Girl to say,

> I tell you with sun pouring down and free for all, I never in my life saw anything like it. I felt I would stand there and just drop my child into their hands, the great Mothers, that's what I saw and will always see as long as I draw breath . . . the suffering of all. I saw mama there, the same bend of back, the sagging belly, the look of sorrow, and of something else, something fierce, and the reason you have a child maybe. (146)

4 Amelia delivers Clara's funeral oration, including:

> Was she a danger? . . . She never stole timber or wheat or made poor flour. She never stole anybody's land or took it for high interest on the mortgage. She never got rich off the labor of others. (146)

5 Amelia delivers the Girl's baby, a girl she names Clara, flanked on one side by the dead Clara and on the other by the mimeograph machine that produced the leaflets demanding milk and iron pills.

All this occurs in *The Girl*'s final ten pages, and, in the lack of a developed class discourse to draw on, it is Le Sueur's desperate last attempt to transmute her Demeter material in the communal consciousness of a proletarian intellectual. In the character of Amelia her Demeter figure is reinscribed as an urban midwife and commune organizer, and the Girl as Persephone has not only made but returned from her descent to Hades, empowered at last to sustain within the commune her mother's great gift of fertility. Amelia delivers the Girl's baby while demanding milk and iron pills for women, and as the baby emerges surrounded by women on the novel's last page, the Girl says,

> A kind of woman's humming was all around me. I saw mama in them all, the bearing and the suffering in us all, their seized bodies, bent bellies hanging, and the ferocity of their guarding. I felt fierce and she seemed to burrow to the nipple as I saw Amelia take the knife she had soaking in alcohol in a beer bottle and cut the cord. (148)

Here struggling up through metaphor and symbol is the actual discourse of an emergent consciousness, and *The Girl* marks the height of Le Sueur's Gramscian effort to create in discourse a concrete consciousness of gender and class.

5

As the thirties passed into the war years when American class and gender oppressions became less traumatic and intertwined, Le Sueur had less immediate occasion to represent their conjunction, and her response to her thirties' window of opportunity did not survive its unresolved conflict between her two Demeters and their respective representations. Her writing of the 1940s and 50s no longer gives the impression of ongoing ferment but of receding echoes. Both versions of her Demeter story disappear, her proletarian and feminist themes become rhetorically perfunctory and faintly elegiac. Her most energetically realized stories, "God Made Little Apples" and "Gone Home," revert to her earlier representation of village life as libidinally repressed. They have nothing to do with communal consciousness.

Then in the McCarthyite 1950s Le Sueur and her children were viciously hounded by the FBI just when her principal publication outlets—*New Masses* and *Mainstream*—also disappeared. For all practical purposes she was silenced until her rediscovery in the 1970s. But from a Gramscian point of view, the feminist movement that now took her up was a middle-class movement of traditional intellectuals, and after a decade in which much of her earlier work was republished, Le Sueur wrote a tantalizingly ambivalent concession to their traditional outlook.

Her 1984 Afterword to *I Hear Men Talking* appeared some fifty years after her Gramscian manifesto in "The Fetish of Being Outside" and is a truly historic sequel. Here Le Sueur explains that she didn't want her works of the 1930s and 40s republished,

> unless they would serve the purpose of illuminating the struggle between the dying class of the oppressors and the rising class of the oppressed. This is the crucial axis of our time, not merely an aesthetic. (Afterword, 237)

That sounds a Gramscian note, as does her statement that the three novellas collected in this volume (which I here assume she also regards as representative) "mark my painful search for a living image that could change my life":

> We are not built in alienation and silence. We must somehow find how to be committed to others, how to express that love which is an act of courage, not of fear, but of bravery and seeing the liberation in each other, that makes us proud and human. I was trying to find

> that action—that love. (Afterword, 237–8)

She then says that she never quite found it, that her stories are "crippled," and that

> I did not know how to make, enlarge, and limn the image of solidarity, *I did not know what the act of transformation was. This was what I did not know and it is now appearing on all horizons*. (Afterword, 239; my emphasis)

But whatever else might have been appearing on all horizons in 1983–4—feminism, environmentalism, multiculturalism—it was not solidarity among the actual people participating in those movements, let alone Gramsci's solidarity of intellectuals with any social formation he (or we) would recognize as a class. Instead, it was just exactly an *image*, a metaphorical abstraction hypothetically suggested by the outpouring of political energy committed to mutually exclusive liberatory movements.

It may well be that in watching women take back the night, environmentalists chain themselves to trees, or lesbians and gays parade in pride, Le Sueur felt as if the fifty-year-old promise of the Minneapolis Teamsters Strike and St. Paul women's commune were being fulfilled. But it wasn't, as we now must know, and meanwhile she was ignoring what she had in fact begun to limn in the aftermath of that strike—solidarity not as an image but as a discursively represented process in a memoir like "I Was Marching" or a novel like *The Girl*. In representing this process she had begun constructing herself as an organic intellectual, then lost the means to continue, and now found herself reinspired by admirers who were innocent of class as either a dimension of experience or category of thought and for whom any distinction between traditional and organic intellectuals would sound like a fairy-tale.

It was then virtually predictable that in the astonishingly renewed energies of her last years, Le Sueur should seek once again in metaphoric condensation the transforming image which she said she had not yet found. Two very different but now complementary works begun in the late 1970s characterize her final phase—the novella *The Dread Road*, published in 1991, and the unfinished prose poem, "The Origins of Corn."[26] In its Whitmanian hyperbole "The Origins of Corn" makes the Midwest village's identity crop a symbol for all existence. Although still subject to capitalist appropriation, Demeter's corn is also the earth's aboriginal source of protein and pollen, the pre-Columbian source of America, the post-Columbian medium of "nation building peoples,"[27] and, among still other things, a force for the liberation of women.[28] Both geologic and historical time are encompassed by a single dialectic for which corn is the symbol, and, fifty years after "Corn Village" noted the absence of community among people who grow corn, "The Origins of Corn" promises, through metaphor, community through corn.

The Dread Road represents metaphorically the destruction of life and community. Here a narrator traveling from Albuquerque to Denver to visit her institutionalized son, who was genetically deformed by nuclear fallout in Nevada, meets on the bus a younger woman carrying a bag that turns out to hold the corpse of her dead baby. These two bond in defiance of a third woman, a prying social worker who suspects they are drug couriers, as the bus passes through Trinidad, where the narrator's grandparents were killed in the Ludlow Massacre. The corpse-carrying younger woman speaks knowingly of Ludlow, and then with the narrator's help she eludes the social worker and police when they arrive in Denver, where the newspapers later report that "A young woman had stood up in the capitol and held a dead baby up to the pure golden dome as if a sacrifice."[29]

The Dread Road's apocalyptic image of deformed and dead children is a fitting counterpart to "The Origin of Corn"'s millennialist image of protein-bearing corn. Together they enable Le Sueur to sustain through her eighth and ninth decades both her capitalism critique and her socialist desire. Yet must we not also say that in the binary exclusiveness required by their reliance on metaphor and symbol, these two works confirm the decline of her Gramscian project to represent the consciousness of the people in a voice they could recognize?

The economic boom and political repression in the United States after World War II effectively destroyed the seedbed for Le Sueur's Gramscian organicism. Her decline paralleled the decline not only of the CPUSA but also of the AFL-CIO and the Democratic Party as forums of discussion and arenas for activism. The social movements that followed have attracted traditional intellectuals but have not coalesced to produce anything they themselves can recognize as a new way of feeling and seeing reality in a nascent alternative hegemony. Where that is concerned, the last fifty years in the United States have brought us virtually back to where we began.

Gramsci wrote as if working-class parties, as seedbeds for organic intellectuals, were irreversibly established within capitalist society. But that has not been the case, and his "advances and retreats, dispersals and regroupings," in which "the loyalty of the masses is often sorely tried," have not been limited to the intellectuals but also have included the working masses and their cultural institutions. Might we not argue that in the United States for the last fifty years, the retreat of the masses has also been a trial to the intellectuals?

Should we then also argue that Gramsci's theory of hegemony, with the function it assigns intellectuals, is finally wishful thinking? A single case study of Meridel Le Sueur is of course not conclusive, but it could be symptomatic. It is hard to imagine, for example, anyone cultivating her role as intellectual in more explicitly Gramscian terms, and while we can imagine a more "organically" integrated intellectual voicing an alternative hegemony more effectively than she did—Subcommandante Marcos, for example—that may not really make a whole lot of difference.

Marcos gives every sign of being a converted traditional intellectual, of having spent years nurturing and being nurtured by a nascent counter-hegemony, of speaking the communal voice of Chiapas in expressing its people's "homogeneity and . . . awareness of its own function," and in producing with that voice a sustained "war of position" within Mexican civil society:

> For a long time, this town has existed where the men are Zapatistas, the women are Zapatistas, the kids are Zapatistas, the chickens are Zapatistas, the stones are Zapatistas, everything is Zapatista. And in order to wipe out the Zapatista Army of National Liberation, they will have to wipe this piece of territory from the face of the earth—not just destroy it but erase it completely because there is always the danger from the dead below.[30]

Yet nobody knows better than the people of Chiapas that they and their nascent hegemony hang in history by a thread. They must live every day with a tragic foreknowledge of possible outcomes far more terrible than Le Sueur's in their struggle to produce a new way of feeling and seeing reality.

While Gramsci does not evince this tragic consciousness, his theory may well require it. Parallel to his distinction between organic and traditional intellectuals are two other distinctions that provide for failure in the struggle for voice, culture, and position: the distinction between "organic" and "conjunctural" politics and the distinction between base and superstructure. Gramsci is honored for his critique of the reductive economism in so many Marxian uses of the base-superstructure metaphor, and then for his conception of hegemony that entails mutual determination rather than unilinear causality from base to superstructure. But unlike many of his modernizers, he does not abandon the base-superstructure distinction. His paired distinctions between organic and traditional intellectuals and organic and conjunctural politics reflect his continuing insistence on the primacy of the base as constituting the terrain on which the superstructure is contested. The organic is identified with the base, the traditional and conjunctural with the superstructure, and their mutual determinations with a historical process through which the conjunctural is transformed into the organic:[31]

> A crisis occurs, sometimes lasting for decades. This exceptional duration means that incurable structural contradictions have revealed themselves . . . and that, despite this, the political forces which are struggling to conserve . . . the existing structure are making every effort to overcome them. These incessant efforts . . . (since no social formation will ever admit that it has been superseded) form the terrain of the "conjunctural," and . . . upon this terrain . . . the forces of opposition organize. These forces seek to demonstrate that the necessary and sufficient conditions already exist *to make possible, and hence imperative,* the accomplishment of certain historical tasks (*imperative, because any falling short before an historical duty increases . . . disorder, and prepares more serious catastrophes*). (177–8, my emphasis)

That final sentence implies a tragic historical duty. Once capitalism has exhausted its possibilities, organic movements have no choice but to enter the terrain of the conjunctural and try to forestall more serious catastrophes by taking any risk necessary to convert conjunctural into organic politics. This effort involves an overdetermined interplay of strategy, tactics, and historical luck, and there is nothing to guarantee its success in any particular circumstances. History is full of its failures and precious debris.

Le Sueur also struggled with the alternative approach of Leninist vanguardism in seeking a Gramscian way into the "sleeping body" of the "unconscious" proletariat. But Leninist praxis is equally subject to overdetermined failure and tragic waste, and I know of no evidence that the vulnerabilities of either Gramscian or Leninist praxis can be remedied by refinements of theory. Instead, all over the world new generations keep putting their judgment on the line in trying one or the other in particular circumstances. North American circumstances being what they are, our generations more often than not attempt the praxis Gramsci theorized. In the United States at the time I write, the fledgling Labor Party has chosen not to engage in the "war of maneuver" of electoral politics but to remain for now a forum of debate in a "war of position" within civil society, and we are also witnessing a mutual reaching out between the labor movement and traditional intellectuals newly committed to this "war of position." Our particular history has produced once again an attempt at counter-hegemony through practical engagement of workers with intellectuals.[32]

But Meridel Le Sueur in her 96 years didn't live to see it. What else could she have done with her valedictory vitality but give up on a new way of seeing reality and revert to a traditional intellectual's binary symbolism in representing (bourgeois) apocalypse and (socialist-feminist) millennium?

6

DENYING THE IMAGINATION IN MARXIAN CULTURAL STUDIES: RAYMOND WILLIAMS AND FREDERIC JAMESON

The Marxian imagination I have tried to identify belongs to human agents struggling to understand and change the world they inherit in which to make their own history. When these people are writers, they stand in the same relation to this world as literary and cultural theorists: their vocation is to change it indirectly through discourse rather than directly through action. Their forms of discourse may be very different from those of theorists; but as I hope I have shown, the difference does not lie in the writers being limited to a political unconscious in contrast to the theorists' magisterial self-awareness. Both have their areas of blindness, whether conscious or unconscious, and the blindness of current cultural theory to the work of imagination is also shared by our most influential Marxists, Raymond Williams and Fredric Jameson. Despite their great differences in other respects, Williams and Jameson both treat the literary work as incapable in itself of the cognitive competence and rhetorical effectiveness that I have ascribed to the writings of James and Le Sueur, Saxton and Shakespeare, Dickens and Lumpkin. In so doing, Williams and Jameson both deny in the name of Marxism not just the political agency of writers and their works, but the long and productive epistemological career of literature itself as a constituting consciousness.[1]

1

Let me begin with Williams, who is for me a baggier but more fertile thinker than the monolithic Jameson. Williams's signal contribution to Marxism is a theory of cultural materialism that rescues the concept of culture from both liberal idealization and Marxian subordination by insisting on a historical progression in which culture, here understood as a whole way of life, passes through emergent, dominant, and residual structures of feeling. The various analyses by which Williams develops this theory seem to me sometimes uneven but always momentous, and even in today's suffocating downpour of publication I would make his great summations—the concluding chapter of *Culture and Society*, the opening chapters of *The Long Revolution*, the essay "Base and Superstructure in Marxian Cultural Theory," and the book *Marxism and Literature*—required reading for both Marxists and exponents of cultural studies.

Yet despite some tantalizing glances toward the imagination I have been expounding, Williams ultimately denies this imagination by denying to the artist any "creative autonomy" to reach outside the structures of feeling through which culture transpires as a historical process. His lifelong effort was to understand culture, with its associated concepts of creativity and imagination, as materially embedded in a historical way of life. But at key junctures his materialism lapses into a lockstep, structuralist empiricism which does not simply embed but also entraps culture and its concepts in that way of life. Although he often shows signs of not wanting to, Williams effectively denies the possibility of reaching directly through imagination the knowledge we always need of any way of life in which art and culture comprise only a part.

Williams's groundbreaking *Culture and Society: 1780–1950* set his lifelong agenda by tracing the modern development of the concept of culture, "with all its complexity of idea and reference," as a shifting conflict between, on the one hand, private, personal cultivation through "a separate body of moral and intellectual activities, and the offering of a court of human appeal," and, on the other hand, a public, communal "whole way of life, not only as a scale of integrity, but as a mode of interpreting all our common experience, and, in this new interpretation, changing it."[2]

He shows among other things how culture, which once meant general human cultivation intrinsic to a common way of life (as with local agriculture for food), was reconceived under the pressure of capitalism as personal cultivation in opposition to capitalism's debased market values, and by that very process was abstracted from a whole way of life and turned into a capitalist specialization. This abstraction extended to such related concepts as creativity and imagination, which now became universal categories, and the thinkers Williams honors in *Culture and Society* were all proposing means to reconnect the human agents of these abstract categories with the concrete experience of a common way of life—Coleridge's Clerisy and Shelley's poet-legislator; Carlyle's organic society and Lawrence's "living homeland"; Tawney's "common culture," Eliot's Christian Society, and the Marxists' ideological superstructure.

Their arguments failed to settle either the meaning of culture or its relation to society, and Williams's project was to recall art, literature, and culture from both their continuing liberal conception as "quasi-metaphysical forms" and their continuing Marxian conception as superstructural forms. In both these conceptions, art and literature, with their attendant creativity and imagination, are abstracted from any overdetermined embedding in a concrete way of life and are invested instead with a "unilinear universalism."[3]

Beginning then with *The Long Revolution* in 1961 and culminating in *Marxism and Literature* in 1977, Williams conducted through his major works a double-barreled critique of liberalism's "imagination" and Marxism's "ideology," for which he came to substitute, respectively, "practical consciousness" and "structures of feeling" as together constituting culture within a whole way of life. His key innovative concept is that of structures of feeling, and in a 1971 essay he explained its origin in his dissatisfaction with superstructural Marxism:

> I came to believe that I had to give up, or at least to leave aside, what I knew as the Marxist tradition: to attempt to develop a different kind of theory of social totality; to see the study of culture as the study of relations between elements in a whole way of life; to find ways of studying structure . . . which could stay in touch with and illuminate particular art-works and forms, but also forms and relations of more general social life; to replace the formula of base and superstructure with the more active idea of a field of mutually if also unevenly determining forces.[4]

Williams's more active idea of mutually determining forces is here the same idea of overdetermination on which I rely so heavily. But where I follow Resnick and Wolff in applying this idea to a temporal process, Williams applies it to a spatial location—a way of life, structure, or field, in the pervasive vocabulary of this passage. His mutually determining forces are structures of feeling, which he defines in *The Long Revolution* as "a particular sense of life, a particular community of experience hardly needing expression," which may not be shared by everyone but is nevertheless "a very deep and very wide possession, in all actual communities, precisely because it is on it that communication depends."[5]

Williams must then incorporate these spatial structures in a temporal interplay of mutual determination, and he does this, first, by replacing traditional Marxism's theory of base and superstructure with Gramsci's more dynamic theory of hegemony, and then by specifying a conflict among structures of feeling within any hegemonic culture. Hegemony for Gramsci is a constantly threatened domination that must be reinforced constantly in an ongoing conflict, and

Williams describes it as follows in *Marxism and Literature*:

> a whole body of practices and expectations, over the whole of living: our senses and assignments of energy, our shaping perceptions of ourselves and our world. It is a lived system of meanings and values— constitutive and constituting— which as they are experienced as practices appear as reciprocally confirming. It thus constitutes . . . a sense of absolute because experienced reality beyond which it is very difficult for most members of the society to move, in most areas of their lives. It is . . . in the strongest sense a "culture," but a culture which also has to be seen as the lived dominance and subordination of particular classes. (*ML,* 110)

In constituting a lived experience of dominance and subordination, hegemonic culture includes the structures of feeling that contend within it.[6] It is a field of conflict, not directly among classes but among these structures of feeling, which Williams now calls "dominant, residual, and emergent." But then he connects these structures in a lockstep progression that I think is alien both to Gramsci's theory and to his own earlier specification of "mutually determining forces" in a fluid temporal process. With structures of feeling, Williams says,

> We are talking about . . . specifically affective elements of consciousness and relationships: not feeling against thought, but thought as felt and feeling as thought: practical consciousness of a present kind, in a living and interrelating continuity. We are then defining these elements as a "structure": as a set, with specific internal relations, at once interlocking and in tension. Yet we are also defining a social experience which is still *in process*, often indeed not recognized as social but taken to be private, idiosyncratic, even isolating, but which . . . has its emergent, connecting, and dominant characteristics, indeed its specific hierarchies. (*ML*, 132; emphasis in text)

Here he connects single instances of Lionel Trilling's "felt awareness of the impact of new circumstances upon old forms of feeling" into structures whose elements interlock in tension. But this tension is then part of a social process apparently limited to contiguous structures—e.g., dominant and emergent—where the internal tension of one structure dynamically produces the ensuing structure as part of a "living and interrelating continuity."

If I understand Williams here, the social process he envisions is not dialectical but empirical: there can be no gap in the material continuum through which a human consciousness spatially rooted in a whole way of life moves across a temporal succession of structures of feeling. Just as the elements of each structure are interlocked internally, the structures themselves are interlinked externally, and this sounds very like an empiricism unwilling to allow crossing that gap by any leap of imagination.

While that may in fact be true for most people in most areas of their lives, where the "sense of absolute because experienced reality" is paramount, what accounts for the other people and other areas? Are those who regularly move beyond the experienced reality of hegemonic culture also limited in doing so only to increments that maintain the continuity of structures of feeling?

Of the three principal contemporary relations of dominance and subordination— class, gender, and race/ethnicity—class is the least palpable and most needs to be experienced through a process of abstraction and a leap of imagination. Meridel Le Sueur tells of a farmworker attending Socialist Party classes in the cornfields after harvest: "One Arkansas hillbilly began to dance when he got the idea of surplus value, that it was not the boss who charitably gave him a job, but that he was the creator of wealth and it was stolen from him."[7] This man's instant passage, evidently from residual to emergent structures of feeling without stopping for dominant, crosses an immaterial gap so huge that he is impelled to respond with a material seizure. Might not his dancing confirm a non-incremental leap of holistic imagination, like Shakespeare's leap into class in *King Lear*, which carried him beyond his hegemonic culture without having to pass through a linked sequence of structures?

2

A parallel question arises from Williams's attempt to ground (and confine?) creativity within his structures of feeling. The opening chapter of *The Long Revolution* is entitled "The Creative Mind," and sixteen years later the closing chapter of *Marxism and Literature* is entitled "Creative Practice," almost as if creativity itself were the subject of Williams's theoretical project. Early in *Marxism and Literature* he recapitulates his argument from *The Long Revolution* that superstructural Marxism, whatever its other differences, coincides with liberal humanism in overlooking the ways in which

> "thinking" and "imagining" are from the beginning social processes (of course including that capacity for "internalization" which is a necessary part of any social process between actual individuals) and that they become accessible only in unarguably physical and material ways: in voices, in sounds made by instruments, in penned or printed writing, in arranged pigments on canvas or plaster, in worked marble or stone. To exclude these material social processes from the material social process is the same error as to reduce all material social processes to merely technical means for some other abstracted "life." (*ML*, 62)

Hence the need for a new term like "practical consciousness," which occurs in *Marxism and Literature* at least a half-dozen times and denotes a single, undifferentiated medium for all our creative activities from metalwork, gardening, and politics to poetry, novel writing, and painting. Practical consciousness is embedded in and arises out of material life. It cannot be abstracted into imagination or ideology, and it is an arena of inevitable conflict within material life—of subjective conflict that also transpires as a social process involving dominant, residual, and emergent structures of feeling.

Then in the concluding chapter of *Marxism and Literature*, Williams elaborates on the difference it actually makes that thinking and imagining become accessible only through a practical consciousness grounded in material life. Here he delineates a hierarchy of artistic practices, beginning with the documentary copying of actual life, which he calls not so much creative in itself as "a consequence of the inherent materiality (and thence objectified sociality) of language"; then ascending to genuine creativity in the "performance of a known model of 'people like this, relations like this'"—a typification which is "the real achievement of most novels and plays"; and ascending finally to "new articulations and formations" that go beyond typification of the already known and are "*necessarily involved with changes in the social formation*" (*ML*, 209; my emphasis).

Then two pages later Williams says that creativity is "inherent most evidently, but not exclusively, in new articulations, and especially those which . . . *reach beyond their time and occasion*" (*ML*, 211; my emphasis). In reaching beyond its time and occasion, practical consciousness can sound at first like the liberal humanist's universal imagination it is meant to replace. But in the context Williams has established this equivalence is impossible because practical consciousness, even when reaching beyond its time and occasion, remains tied to changes in the social formation with their interlinked progression of structures of feeling.

That is of course often true, and may account for the perennial Marxian example of Balzac, whom we regard as prescient in representing the new processes and sentiments of capitalism in *Père Goriot* and *Lost Illusions*. But there can be different forms of even prescient response to social change, and correspondingly different forms, degrees, or effects of reaching beyond one's time and occasion. Shakespeare, Dickens, Burke, and Le Sueur, in their works that I have discussed, can all be described like Balzac as ahead of their time, but all in different ways, and Williams has no way to relate their differences to structures of feeling. From what we can reasonably surmise, Shakespeare had less discernible evidence to go on than Balzac, while Le Sueur had more, in responding to contemporary changes in class structures, processes and sentiments. But Shakespeare's response is arguably more prescient than Balzac's, Le Sueur's less prescient than either of theirs, and these differences are nowhere linked to structures of feeling that register change in a social formation. They are personal differences, not only in a writer's acuity of awareness but also in her capacity to articulate her awareness in the form of her art. Might Shakespeare have been ahead of his time, not just by responding precociously like Balzac to change in the social formation, but by the internal momentum of his personal imagination in its material engagement with his story?

This material engagement generates its own capacity for abstraction, and Williams's hierarchy of creative practice—from literal reproduction to typification to new articulation reaching beyond its time and occasion—is also a hierarchy of levels of abstraction. Yet as the level of abstraction rises, the creator's immersion in sounds made by instruments, pigments on canvas, or penned words may in fact enable her, in and of itself, to produce a holistic knowledge that reaches beyond any specific involvement in a social formation or its structures of feeling. On the one hand, Shakespeare's breakthrough in *King Lear* to an imagination of class is accompanied by a one-time deformation of his Aristotelian plot in which we cannot tell which is the chicken and which the egg: the material innovations produced by pen on paper are both cause and effect of Shakespeare's horrified imagination of capitalist rapacity as represented by Edmund. On the other hand, Meridel Le Sueur's lifelong commitment to overreaching a class process nakedly visible in her social formation could not by itself bring her securely to an imagination of class in the material practice of her penned writing. Originating neither exclusively in language nor in any particular structure of feeling, this imagination entails a process of abstraction induced by material practice but then proceeding on its own, whether beyond or still within its time and occasion.[8] In so doing, it finally shares with the humanist imagination an epistemological capacity that does not depend on a "metaphysic of subjectivity" or a "unilinear universalism."

Let me illustrate finally Williams's empirical confinement of practical consciousness to the social formation and its structures of feeling by returning to Dickens, with whom I began and who is also a recurring example for Williams throughout his work. Where Lionel Trilling in his essay on *Little Dorrit* will not recognize Dickens's class narrative, Williams will not recognize Dickens's capacity to produce any such master narrative. For him Dickens's practical consciousness, even when reaching ahead of its time, can only illustrate what Williams calls in *The Long Revolution* "the connection between the popular structure of feeling and that used in the literature of the time" (*LR*, 67).

In *Marxism and Literature* he describes this connection as follows:

> Early Victorian ideology . . . specified the exposure caused by poverty or by debt or by illegitimacy as social failure or deviation; the contemporary structure of feeling, meanwhile, in the new semantic figures of Dickens, of Emily Brontë, and others, specified exposure and isolation as a *general* condition, and poverty, debt, and illegitimacy as its connecting instances. An alternative ideology, relating such exposure to the nature of the social order, was only later generally formed. (*ML*, 134; emphasis in text)

Here I think Williams reveals inadvertently, through his suddenly improvised distinction between ideology and structure of feeling, the limitation he has imposed on practical consciousness as a substitute for imagination. The material penning of words which is the work of practical consciousness, and which also incorporates thought as felt and feeling as thought, is nevertheless here insufficient to enter the realm of ideology, which evidently requires a still different consciousness.

A three-step progression is laid out in this passage—from early Victorian ideology to its linked structure of feeling that is both contemporary and new, and then to an alternative ideology later to be formed, evidently through a further interlinked progression. Dickens and Brontë may be as original as you like in articulating a structure of feeling that advances beyond contemporary ideology, yet their advance is limited to a single step and cannot by itself reach a comprehension of the whole social order. It cannot constitute but only prepare the ground—and then wait—for this ideological comprehension to form through some other agency at some future time.[9]

Williams's great Dickensian example is then predictably not mine of *Little Dorrit*, through whose holistic point of entry Dickens enters immediately and directly into an imagination of class, but *Dombey and Son*, through whose isolated passages Dickens's practical consciousness episodically articulates new structures of feeling in response to the industrialization and urbanization which are no more than indirect conditions of capitalism's class process. *Dombey and Son* is the focus of Williams's thirty-page analysis of Dickens in *The English Novel from Dickens to Lawrence* (later recapitulated in *The Country and the City*), where his point of departure is the 1840s generation of British novelists who produced "a new kind of consciousness" devoted to "the exploration of community; the substance and meaning of community." He identifies Dickens's contribution to this new consciousness by an inventory of quotations, most but not all from "the radically innovative *Dombey and Son*,"[10] which are connected not by the pattern they make in one novel but by the structures of feeling they share with popular culture:

> The central case we have to make is that Dickens could write a new kind of novel—fiction uniquely capable of realising a new kind of reality—just because he shared with the new urban popular culture certain decisive experiences and responses. (*EN*, 31–2)

In *Dombey and Son*, these experiences and responses are principally a) to the city as a place of "hurrying seemingly random passing of men and women, each heard in some fixed phrase, seen in some fixed expression"—and thus also as a place where "the real and inevitable relationships . . . of any human society" are newly "obscured, complicated, mystified, by the sheer rush and noise and miscellaneity of this new and complex social order"; b) to the building of the Railroad as creating both "the disorder of change" and "a kind of new order that is made to emerge from it"; and c) to a change in the character of moral analysis itself, in which society is no longer a background for the drama of virtue and vice but is itself "the creator of virtues and vices" (*EN*, 32–33 passim, 42–44 passim).

Without inordinate quotation I cannot do justice either to Dickens's insight and power in the passages Williams analyzes or to the brilliance of Williams's analyses. Suffice it to say that for the passages he has chosen his conclusion is compelling: that Dickens produces in these passages "an advance in consciousness" which is also "very clearly a gain . . . in fictional method" (*EN*, 40).

But when Williams goes on to claim that "Dickens's morality, his social criticism, is in the form of his novels" (*EN*, 48) and also that this form involves "a whole way of seeing" (*EN*, 59), he elevates what is actually in the novels a sporadic way of seeing within a localized structure of feeling to the form of the work as a whole. The final 200-odd pages of *Dombey and Son*, in which the Carker–Edith melodrama is played out and Florence Dombey is sentimentally reunited with her miraculously surviving lover and miraculously softened father, offer very little evidence of a new way of seeing, or an advance in consciousness that is also a gain in fictional method. Williams in fact has ascribed this advance only to earlier passages—e.g., those depicting Florence's flight through the city or the social and moral "earthquake" of building the Railroad. But the "whole way of seeing" implied by such genuinely innovative passages is in fact suppressed by the form of the novel as a whole, which thereby keeps from itself the knowledge of class that *Little Dorrit* attains. This surely must help explain why so many readers feel disappointed, not to say betrayed, by *Dombey and Son*'s overbearing closure in Dickensian melodrama and sentimentality.

It is hard to imagine anyone saying of this novel what Shaw said of *Little Dorrit*— that it is more subversive than *Das Kapital* and that he is now a revolutionist because he read *Little Dorrit* as a boy. Not only does *Little Dorrit* depict poverty and debt as connecting instances of general exposure and in so doing articulate a new structure of feeling. It then proceeds in its total configuration to suppress its Dickensian melodrama and sentimentality in the process of relating this exposure to the nature of the social order. When the villain Rigaud says at the end, "Effectively, Sir . . . Society sells itself and sells me; and I sell Society," he is summing up the entire plot implicating its major characters; and when following soon upon this statement Amy Dorrit and Arthur Clennam walk down together into "the roaring streets," in the novel's famous final paragraph, they are not simply duplicating Florence Dombey's equally famous flight through the city, although Williams has earlier equated the two passages. The material penning of Arthur's and Amy's descent now embodies, not a local structure of feeling in response to the urbanization incidental to capitalism, but a general knowledge acquired by this novel in the total course of its material practice—what Williams has called an alternative ideology yet to be formed—in which the reality of the social order is seen as the reality of its class process.

In failing to reach *Little Dorrit*'s knowledge of class, *Dombey and Son* is not only "less Marxist" but also in this instance a lesser novel, and here I think is another dimension of Williams's empiricist subsumption of literature to sociology. For all his strictures on the imagination and the aesthetic as quasi-metaphysical categories, he often acknowledges a difference between better and worse literary works. Writing in *The Long Revolution* of the novelists of the 1840s, he distinguishes "the best work of the period" from "the less good and bad," and he also says that "Thackeray, Dickens, and Charlotte Brontë survive on strict literary merit, but we see that their best works have carried inferior works that in other authors would have vanished" (*LR*, 58–9). Here his criteria for literary merit, whatever they might be, bear no evident relation to his conceptions of practical consciousness and structures of feeling.

Might not *Dombey and Son*, for all its formal innovation where structures of feeling are concerned, nevertheless be an inferior work where literary merit is concerned, and owe its survival to *Bleak House*, *Little Dorrit*, and *Our Mutual Friend*? Many would say so. While I would no more equate automatically a total class narrative than a local structure of feeling with literary merit, I have also tried to show how Marxism's master narrative, when it does become a novel's point of entry, can produce through its form a knowledge and power unavailable to forms defined by ways of seeing apart from what is ultimately seen. The formal struggles I have ascribed to Shakespeare and Dickens—and to James, Le Sueur, Lumpkin, and Saxton— are defined by what these writers are themselves trying (and trying not) to see. They are struggles toward what liberal humanism called a "vision," yet a vision no longer metaphysical but now historically specific. It is the vision of class that has sustained Marxism itself through 150 years of tragic witness to a whole succession of structures of feeling—most recently those whose names are prefixed by "post"—and its literary embodiments are central to that witness. They need to be reappropriated in their centrality both by Marxian theory and the scholarship of cultural materialism, and Raymond Williams's empiricism,[11] for all the help of one kind it gives us in understanding culture, is also a barrier to that appropriation.

3

Williams's structuralist empiricism precludes the Marxian imagination I have been expounding, and so does Fredric Jameson's superstructuralist idealism. In this respect a pivotal text of Jameson for me is "On Interpretation: Literature as a Socially Symbolic Act," his 100-page opening chapter in *The Political Unconscious*. There he completes a process, begun in *Marxism and Form*, of turning history into teleology—"the formal effects of . . . an 'absent cause'"[12]—and culture into epiphenomenon—"symbolic messages transmitted . . . by the coexistence of various sign systems which are themselves traces . . . of modes of production" (*PU*, 76)—despite his immensely learned effort to swaddle the appearance of doing so. *The Political Unconscious* begins with the slogan, "Always historicize!" (*PU*, 9), and any Marxist has to love that. But by the final paragraphs of "On Interpretation," Jameson is newly spelling "History" with a capital *H* and describing it as "the experience of Necessity" and the "ground and untranscendable horizon" (*PU*, 103) of all human praxis. To the superstructuralist foundation for that description a fellow Marxist may well take exception.[13]

The exception I take is, first, to Jameson's conception of history as a fixed spatial terrain determined by the mode of production rather than a structured temporal process overdetermined by the mode of production; and second, to his conception of Marxism as solely able to map this terrain. Not only does he regularly abstract history into metaphors of ground and horizon, sector and sediment, "diachronic construct" and "diachronic sequence"; he also claims for Marxism the exclusive capacity to interpret everything within the space thus marked out. Marxism as politics subsumes other politics like feminism because "sexism and the patriarchal are to be grasped as the sedimentation . . . of forms of alienation specific to the oldest mode of production of human history, with its division of labor between men and women" (*PU* 99–100). Equally, Marxism as hermeneutic subsumes other hermeneutics like Freudianism because "The conditions of possibility of psychoanalysis become visible . . . only when you begin to appreciate the extent of psychic fragmentation since the beginnings of capitalism . . . with its instrumental reorganization of the subject just as much as of the outside world" (*PU*, 62).

Jameson goes on to argue that feminism for its own sake must seek to abolish the commodity form, and that Freudian desire is a utopian impulse produced specifically by capitalism, so that both possess what he has earlier called a "sectoral validity" (*PU*, 10) within the total space governed by Marxism. But he also fails to mention, let alone engage, alternative arguments surely familiar to someone of his learning—that patriarchy did not arise simply (or even mainly) from the sexual division of labor, or that the psychic fragmentation Freud identified in the works of Sophocles and Shakespeare predates capitalist instrumentalism—that could give feminism or Freudianism an effectiveness and jurisdiction independent of Marxism. Such arguments lead to a theory of overdetermination among theories themselves—what Walter A. Davis calls "dialectical pluralism"[14]—in which Marxism is only one entry to a complex historical process that Jameson reduces to a "sequence of modes of production" (*PU*, 75) with their governing "ideolog[ies] of form" (*PU,* 98).

Although he regularly attempts to finesse this version of base and superstructure, from his early argument for Althusser's "expressive causality" as a Marxian alternative to Spengler's and Taine's (with its reliance on the medieval hermeneutic of levels of meaning) to his later claim that all previous modes of production are simultaneously contending within capitalism, these do not extricate Jameson from his underlying assumption that modes of production also produce an exclusive and governing "content of form" (*PU*, 99) for works of art and literature. This assumption is clearly articulated in *Marxism and Form* and is then evident throughout Jameson's practical criticism— in the chapters on magical narratives, Balzac, Gissing, and Conrad that follow "On Interpretation" in *The Political Unconscious*, and the riffs on Van Gogh/Warhol, Doctorow, and the Westin Bonaventure Hotel in "Postmodernism, or, The Cultural Logic of Late Capitalism."

In *Marxism and Form*'s concluding 100-page chapter ("Towards Dialectical Criticism"), Jameson's conception of art as superstructural reflection clearly anticipates that of "On Interpretation." Here he claims that

> the adequation of object to subject or of form to content can exist as an imaginative possibility only where . . . it has been concretely realized in social life itself, so that formal realizations, as well as formal defects, are . . . the signs of some deeper *corresponding* social and historical configuration which it is the task of criticism to explore. (my emphasis)[15]

The artist's role in realizing this imaginative possibility is altogether determined. Neither her formal actualizations nor their defects lie within the province of her individual imagination, since for Jameson as for so many followers of Foucault, the artist, unlike the theoretician, cannot transcend the hegemonic relations of power and ideology dictated (for Jameson) by the mode of production:

> the logic of artistic content, for which the artist himself is merely an instrument, . . . using the accidents of his personal life as the very element of its own formal research, [develops] through him . . . according to its own intrinsic laws. (*MF*, 329)

"The logic of content" is a recurrent, attention-calling phrase in *Marxism and Form*, and it anticipates such phrases as "the content of form" and "ideology of form" in *The Political Unconscious*, "the cognitive aesthetics of third-world literature" in "Third World Literature in the Era of Multinational Capital,"[16] and "the cultural logic of late capitalism" and "cognitive mapping" in "Postmodernism: or, The Cultural Logic of Late Capitalism." In all these monologic, profoundly undialectical formulations, what Jameson calls "the active presence within the text of a number of discontinuous and heterogeneous formal processes" indicates, not an overdetermined dialectic subject to the writer's active purpose, but rather the inert layers of "sedimented content" (*PU*, 99) whose inexorable logic embeds the helpless writer in a "diachronic sequence":

> That Flaubert is *sui generis* is to say nothing; but that he is no longer Balzac, that he is not yet Zola, and this in a host of determinate ways, is to articulate the structures inherent in and constitutive of the novel of Flaubert. (*MF*, 314–15)

Jameson's most productive contribution to scholarship lies in his brilliant readings—of novels, paintings, buildings—that illustrate this kind of generalization. His now famous reading of the Westin Bonaventure Hotel as a postmodern text is for me the most compelling of these,[17] but it is also of a piece with any number of similarly "Eureka!" readings of, for example, Hemingway's style, magical narratives, or Van Gogh's "Peasant Shoes." Quotations out of context can hardly do these justice, but here is at least a sampler:

1 Beginning with the assertion that Hemingway's "deepest subject" is not "courage, love, and death," but "simply the writing of a certain type of sentence," Jameson elaborates as follows:

> Writing, now conceived as a *skill*, is then assimilated to the other skills of hunting and bullfighting . . . which project a total image of man's . . . all-absorbing technical participation in the outside world . . . The Hemingway cult of *machismo* . . . satisfies the Protestant work ethic at the same time that it glorifies leisure; it reconciles the . . . most life-giving impulses toward wholeness with a status quo in which only sports allow you to feel alive and undamaged. (*MF*, 411–12; emphasis in text)

2 In the Italian society of the period [i.e., of Manzoni's *I Promessi Sposi*], strongly marked by the new Enlightenment values but far less secularized than the most advanced post-revolutionary states, the concept of Providence still provides an adequate theoretical mediation between the salvational logic of the romance narrative and the nascent sense of historicity imposed by the social dynamic of capitalism. Where, in other situations, such as that of Stendhal, this compromise concept is unavailable, we observe a curious oscillation . . . between the archaic and the secular. (*PU*, 132)

3 Beginning with the assertion that the "initial raw materials" of "Peasant Shoes" are "to be grasped simply as the whole object world of agricultural misery," Jameson asks,

> How is it then that in Van Gogh such things as apple trees explode into a hallucinatory surface of colour . . . ? I will briefly suggest . . . that the willed and violent transformation of a drab peasant object world into the most glorious materialization of pure colour . . . is to be seen as a Utopian gesture: as an act of compensation which ends up producing a whole new Utopian realm of the senses which it now reconstitutes for us as . . . part of some new division of labor in the body of capital, some new fragmentation of the emergent sensorium which replicates the . . . divisions of capitalist life at the same time that it seeks in precisely such fragmentation a desperate Utopian compensation for them.[18]

Whatever else may be true of Hemingway, Manzoni, Stendhal, or Van Gogh, all of this is stunningly true, and it shows them implicated up to their ears in the ideological dynamics of capitalism. But for Jameson this is also the entire truth, and it keeps them trapped in ideology with only the recourse of utopian compensation while also perhaps cutting off their ears. Jameson calls (among other things) Van Gogh's color utopian, modernist architecture utopian, Freudian desire utopian, Balzac's secretaryship of French society utopian. The utopian is for him a fixed slot built into the superstructure, which can then be filled by any and every attempt, however desperate or destructive, to compensate for capitalism's success in reifying our consciousness and making us the instruments of its logic of content.

Marxism must therefore supplement its traditional "negative hermeneutic" of "ideological analysis" with a new "positive hermeneutic" of utopian "decipherment" (*PU*, 296), and Jameson formulates this innovation in the concluding chapter of *The Political Unconscious*, "The Dialectic of Utopia and Ideology." There he explains how "the process of totalization outlined in our opening chapter offers no way out of this the 'labor and suffering of the negative'" (*PU*, 284)—i.e., the labor and suffering entailed by our subjection to ideology. The "desperate compensation" elicited by this suffering can then only take the form of "Utopian gesture" in need of deciphering. In Van Gogh and modernist architecture it is to be deciphered as compensation for the fragmented capitalist sensorium, and in Freudian desire and Balzac's secretaryship it is to be deciphered as compensation for the fragmented capitalist community. For Jameson, class conflict automatically produces a sense of community within each of the conflicting groups, exploiters as well as exploited. But until it can be universalized across both groups, this solidarity must remain "Utopian insofar as it expresses the unity of a collectivity." Meanwhile it can function as a "*figure* for the ultimate concrete collective life of an achieved Utopian or classless society" (*PU*, 291; emphasis in text).

In Jameson's "theory of immanent Utopianism," as Eric Schocket calls it in an unpublished paper, the utopian gesture functions as compensation for the fragmenting of those "traditional social forms, human relations, or religious systems" that Jameson also calls "unities." These unities are fragmented by the process of reification intrinsic to capitalism:

> these now isolated broken bits and pieces of the older unities acquire a . . . semiautonomous coherence which, not merely a reflex of capitalist reification and rationalization, also in some measure serves to compensate for the dehumanization of experience reification brings with it, and to rectify the otherwise intolerable effects of the new process. (*PU*, 63)

But as Schocket observes, "not every 'subtextual' longing is for a lost unity; not all unities are worth longing for," so that no "Utopian gesture" can be *ipso facto* either admirable or satisfying as a form of compensation or rectification.[19] It is then not surprising that for Jameson, the utopian impulse is always either "desperate" or "repressed," and its decipherment figural rather than literal, because none of us individually can overcome by direct reflection the tense subjection to ideology that triggers our utopian gestures. We cannot learn to long on our own for something we can know as assuredly worth longing for.

The artist subject to spasmodic utopian gesture within ideology is incapable of holistic utopian reflection beyond ideology,[20] and Jameson characterizes as a Marxian "mirage" the vision of

> a moment in which the individual subject would be somehow fully conscious of his or her determination by class and would be able to square the circle of ideological conditioning by . . . the taking of thought . . . [In] the Marxian system, only a collective unity— whether that of . . . the proletariat, or of its "organ of consciousness," the revolutionary party— can achieve this transparency; the individual subject is always positioned within the social totality (and this is the sense of Althusser's insistence on the *permanence* of ideology). (*PU*, 283; emphasis in text)

Here he closes the teleological circle opened in *Marxism and Form* by invoking a "Marxian system" wherein class consciousness is determined separately from ideology by the mode of production as deus ex machina. In this determination, the individual can't take thought because she is "always positioned within the social totality" governed by ideology. Class awareness then cannot be created among individuals moved to thought by concrete historical struggle in which a new consciousness is wrested from ideology—the political struggle of, say, Thompson's weavers, artisans, and utopians, or the cultural struggle of Shakespeare and Arnow, Dickens and James, Saxton and Le Sueur. Instead, class awareness is created by the fiat of Marxism, which guarantees it from a transideological realm accessible to the theorist but not to the weaver or novelist—Althusser's "scientific" realm as understood by Jameson to be the realm of History as Necessity.

4

In his later and hugely influential essay, "Postmodernism, or, The Cultural Logic of Late Capitalism," Jameson's Marxism then comes full circle in his argument for "cognitive mapping" as a necessary step beyond utopian decipherment in enabling us "to grasp our positioning as individual and collective subjects [i.e., our class position] and regain a capacity to act and struggle" (92).

His stated purpose in this essay is to identify postmodernism "not as a style, but rather as a cultural dominant" whose logic of content requires us both to expand our sensorium and to "reflect more adequately on the most effective forms of any radical cultural politics today" (56–7 passim). Jameson's attempt at more adequate reflection then produces the essay's concluding proposal for cognitive mapping, to succeed the utopian decipherment which itself replaced ideological analysis, as the necessary form of "a new radical cultural politics" (89). This proposal is offered, however, with a striking lack of confidence:

> The new political art—*if it is indeed possible at all*—will have to hold to the truth of postmodernism, that is to say, to its fundamental object—the world space of multinational capital—at the same time at which it achieves a breakthrough to some *as yet unimaginable* new mode of representing this last. . . . The political form of postmodernism, *if there ever is any*, will have as its vocation the invention and projection of a global cognitive mapping, on a social as well as a spatial scale. (92; my emphasis)

Those are the final words of "Postmodernism," and while they can perhaps be read simply as exhortation to take postmodernism seriously before it's too late, they can also be taken as a dead end for the superstructural Marxism on which Jameson has relied throughout the works I have discussed.

Why shouldn't it be possible for postmodernism to produce a political art as previous ideologies of form have done? I think it's because Jameson's postmodernism, as distinguished from the realism he associates with early capitalism's "machine production of steam-driven motors," and from the modernism he associates with middle capitalism's "electric and combustion motors," is now associated with the "nuclear-powered apparatuses" of late capitalism (78)[21] and is thus endowed with a newly irresistible power to colonize our minds and reify our consciousness.[22]

This postmodernism, like the "History" of "On Interpretation," conflates physical with metaphorical space and then supplants "History" in occupying totally both kinds of space. For Jameson the "world space of multinational capital" is both the earth itself and a "social space" so thoroughly permeated by postmodern culture that the "critical distance" (91), which once gave left politics "the possibility of positioning the cultural act outside the massive Being of capital," (87) has been erased. Hence the need for cognitive mapping, from inside this massive Being, to supplant the utopian gesture formerly made from that critical distance.

Space is Jameson's signature mode of cognition, and among the many cultural figures and forms by which he identifies postmodernism—Warhol, Cage, Burroughs, Godard; pop art, punk rock, photorealism; *nouveau roman* and "the aesthetics of textuality" (54)—architecture remains foremost. He says that "it was indeed from architectural debates that my own conception of postmodernism first began to emerge" and then that "architecture remains the privileged aesthetic language" of postmodernism (79). Focusing on this language, he distinguishes between the postmodern architecture that requires a politics of cognitive mapping and the modernist architecture of utopian gesture. Both deliberately set themselves apart from the "urban squalor" (76) of their surroundings. But where modernist architecture does so as a utopian gesture of repudiation, postmodern architecture does so as a "vernacular" gesture of distilled replication. In its "aesthetic populism" (14), the Westin Bonaventure Hotel

> does not wish to be part of the city, but rather its equivalent and its replacement or substitute . . . [T]his disjunction from the surrounding city is very different from that of the great monuments of the International Style . . . whose gesture radically separates the new Utopian space of the modern from the degraded and fallen city fabric which it thereby repudiates . . . The Bonaventure, however, is content to "let the fallen city fabric continue to be in its being" . . . ; no further effects, no larger protopolitical Utopian transformation, is either expected or desired. (81)

What postmodernism expects and desires, instead of utopian transformation, is an acceptance of its

> imperative to grow new organs, to expand our sensorium and our body to some new, *as yet unimaginable, perhaps ultimately impossible*, dimensions. (80; my emphasis)

Jameson does not ask whether this expanded sensorium would facilitate or preempt cognitive mapping. Yet if a new sensorium makes political transformation irrelevant, what can be the purpose of cognitive mapping as the "new radical cultural politics" appropriate to that sensorium? If in the hyperspace of postmodernism we are subject as never before to a hyperideology that Althusser says is permanent, how could *any* cultural politics ever again make us aware of our class position and enable us to regain our capacity to struggle?

It may then be a blessing that Jameson finds both an expanded sensorium and cognitive mapping "perhaps ultimately impossible," or we might be joining Fukuyama at the End of History. Instead, Jameson has brought us perhaps to the end of History as Necessity. His rejection in *The Political Unconscious* of "the taking of thought," as a means to become aware of our class position, has now led by his own logic to the dead end of a metaphorical space in whose cognitive mapping he shows no practical confidence. He has demarcated this space so as first to make utopian gesture irrelevant, and then cognitive mapping "perhaps ultimately impossible" despite its newly indispensable vocation, and thus in effect to talk himself out of his own alternatives to the taking of thought in what Davis calls "a Marxism without Guarantees."[23] He has enacted the entropy of the political unconscious and left us little to lose by turning to alternative Marxian theories which his massive presence has crowded to the margins of academic discourse. And in such theories as Resnick and Wolff's overdetermination and point of entry, or Davis's "situated subjectivity" (189) and "existent reflection" (202), we can again find warrant for taking direct thought of our class position from the struggles we must inevitably conduct from inside the belly of the Beast.

5

In simultaneously seeking and resisting this class awareness in and through their aesthetic forms, the writers I have discussed are engaged precisely in the taking of thought. As their formal categories and customary practices break down, they not only illustrate but also contend with their subjection to the ideology of form, and in that contention sometimes proceed directly to class thought without passing through the spasm of utopian gesture. Where the awareness of class is concerned, their struggle regularly produces Resnick and Wolff's conflicting points of entry among adjacent works— Dickens's *Hard Times* and *Little Dorrit*; James's *The Princess Casamassima* and *The Bostonians*; Le Sueur's *I Hear Men Talking* and *The Girl*—so that we cannot say of them what Jameson says of Flaubert (and, by implication, the Westin Bonaventure Hotel), that to specify how he is no longer Balzac but not yet Zola is to specify what is constitutive of the novel of Flaubert. Instead, we can see these writers and their works as constituted by an overdetermined, dialectical response to their engagement with their situated subjectivity.[24] Our purpose in reading them can then become Davis's purpose: "to uncover history as it exists for a conflicted subject engaged in the effort to mediate historical contradiction through recourse to thought" (194).

That at any rate has been my purpose in this book, where I have also tried to show how "thought" can transpire as Lionel Trilling says it can, in and through literary structure and affect—in an aesthetic form that embraces the sociological rather than a sociological form that erases the aesthetic. We are indebted to Raymond Williams and Fredric Jameson for pioneering the rescue of cultural scholarship from an artificially depoliticized humanism; each in his way shows beyond doubt how the work of art is historically contingent and inescapably political. But they and their followers have ended up by affirming an artificially dehumanized cultural politics that leads to its own dead end. In so doing, they invite us to step back and redefine humanism rather than renounce it. One of Sartre's essays is entitled "Existentialism Is a Humanism," implying there are more than one, and surely one subtext of this book is that Marxism is also a humanism. That is why it is able finally to produce in some works I have discussed a tragic knowledge all its own.

7
CODA: IMAGINING HISTORY IN *THE POISONWOOD BIBLE*

During the years I have been writing this book Barbara Kingsolver has emerged as a leading American novelist, and her achievement in *The Poisonwood Bible* renews in American culture the Marxian imagination I have been stalking in my book. I have argued that this imagination regularly finds expression in a narrative of overdetermination and is often marked by tragedy. But while *The Poisonwood Bible* is clearly a novel of overdetermination, it is just as clearly not a tragedy, and in both these respects it is most like *Little Dorrit* among the works I have discussed. Yet despite their fine comic energy, neither do these two novels compose finally as comedies, and where Northrop Frye would no doubt have called them universal works of irony and winter, here I want to call them novels of contingent history as Marxism's great alternative to tragedy.

The history they involve is not Lukács's typified history of objective reality in its internal self-movement, to be abstracted from the narrative by a reader already equipped with Marxian theory by other discourse practices. It is instead the history represented by a discourse practice able in itself to equip a Marxian reader, just like those other practices, and more movingly and lastingly than many.

The Poisonwood Bible's denouement, in which two white American sisters, Rachel and Leah Price, continue their vastly different lives in the Africa where their missionary family's catastrophe occurred, parallels Dickens's denouement in which Amy Dorrit and Arthur Clennam descend into London's "roaring streets" after their family catastrophes in *Little Dorrit*. Both narratives reach closure by maintaining their commitment to the open-ended, overdetermined history, both personal and social, which they have so assiduously spent themselves in representing. Their densely interwoven determinations preempt us from abstracting them into canonical forms like tragedy and comedy, and their density derives from both writers' bonding with their audience through immersion in the discourses of popular culture.

1

Like Dickens, Kingsolver shares with her audience a range of interests and feelings that enables her to engage and challenge this audience in a variety of popular forms and styles. She has published novels, poetry, short stories, and many kinds of journalism in the *New York Times Magazine*, *Smithsonian*, *Parenting*, *Architectural Digest*, and *Natural History* (not to mention the Denver *Post* and Tucson *Weekly*), on subjects as diverse as parenting, joining a health club, divorce, molecular genetics, and fencing one's property. She has covered a strike as Dickens did at Preston, she has performed in a rock band comprised of writers raising money for literacy, and she has saturated *The Poisonwood Bible* with a bubbling compound of sit-com argot and Biblical allusion.

Her audience's response has also been Dickensian. During the year and more while it was on the bestseller lists, *The Poisonwood Bible* became a selection of the Oprah Winfrey Book Club; it prompted the reprinting of Kingsolver's earlier books in a boxed set; it produced a website, *kingsolver.com*; and it made no more dent than Dickens often made in American university English departments, where Toni Morrison and Don DeLillo still reign supreme among contemporary novelists.

Also like Dickens, Kingsolver is not in the first place a social or political novelist but a prodigy of comic invention who takes all kinds of risks in energizing the language while also imbuing her stories with a loving respect for ordinary people. It's true that her earlier novels exhibit an un-Dickensian, overt political awareness loosely reminiscent of the American proletarian novelists. But the political motifs of these early novels are liberal commonplaces now shared by millions, like Dickens's structures of feeling, and except for *Pigs in Heaven*, these novels keep their politics in the background where it cannot participate in constituting the narrative as it does for Burke, Le Sueur, Lumpkin, and Saxton. In *The Bean Trees* a convenient role is played by a Central American refugee couple and the Arizona woman who provides them a safehouse, and in *Animal Dreams* the protagonist's sister is killed by the *contras* while doing volunteer work offstage in Nicaragua. Only in *Pigs in Heaven*, where the protagonist must be reconciled through a child custody dispute with her dispossessed counterpart in the Cherokee Nation, do the political and the familial mutually determine each other, and in that respect *Pigs in Heaven* does faintly anticipate *The Poisonwood Bible.*

Even so, *The Poisonwood Bible* comes out of nowhere in Kingsolver's development. Where Dickens had to be pulled by his art from a local structure of feeling to a holistic imagination of class in a graduated progression that only climaxes in *Little Dorrit*, Kingsolver was propelled exponentially to gender/-

class/race as her holistic point of entry by the explosive political energy bottled up in her earlier novels. *The Poisonwood Bible*, like the *Eroica* Symphony, is astonishing not only in itself but in its giant leap of personal imagination beyond anything you could have predicted from its writer's earlier work. Here I want to delineate briefly its pattern of overdetermination, since my argument on that topic is by now familiar, and then to evoke the literary form that I think it shares with *Little Dorrit*.

2

My immensely well-read friend Marlene Longenecker says *The Poisonwood Bible* is the first novel she has read about the experience of being white, and to that I would add (not that she wouldn't) being also an American woman whose family patriarch forces her to grow up in an imperial colony now being remobilized, through the CIA's murder of Patrice Lumumba, for renewed capitalist expropriation. The mother and four daughters who share the first-person narration of *The Poisonwood Bible* find themselves in the Congo at the insistence of their *paterfamilias*, a missionary bent on baptizing the heathen in a river habitat of crocodiles, and whenever not proselytizing is also bent on cultivating a demonstration garden of American crops by American methods despite the advice of natives who know their own soil and climate.

His effort to impose his way of life becomes only the more crazed the more it is frustrated, until his wife and daughters, as they experience the destruction he is sowing everywhere, have no choice but to break out of their Southern Baptist female subservience. Then in a ramifying web of overdetermination, these women's struggles to free themselves from their lord and master require them to take individual responsibility for their white presence in Africa, and also for their role in the class process by which King Leopold's Ghost is returning to the Congo in the shape of Mobutu.[1] "You'll say," says the guilt-ridden mother to the reader at the outset, "I walked across Africa with my wrists unshackled, and now I am one more soul walking free in a white skin, wearing some thread of the stolen goods: cotton or diamonds, freedom at the very least, prosperity."[2]

The novel's representation of overdetermination includes as a matter of course the Price family's relations with the natives, where, for example, Leah, who has fallen in love with the exquisitely tattooed village schoolteacher, also insists on joining the village hunt and thereby challenges the native gender tradition from within in a manner quite opposite to that in which her father challenges the native religion from without; or where Rachel is courted by the village chief who covets her beauty for his tattooed harem but who also wishes to relieve her family's hunger by one mouth through an act of philanthropy for his Christian antagonist; or where the native outcasts within their own religion are the ones most responsive to the proselytizer's Christianity. Yet for all these and other cross-cultural complexities, *The Poisonwood Bible*'s most deeply affecting structural overdeterminations involve the relations—personal, political, and rhetorical—among the Price family women through whose overlapping narratives the tale is actually told.

These women break free of their patriarch in ways that define their differences as unique and often opposed personalities. Their bodies, minds, and voices are different, their purposes become different, their outcomes are very different, and the richness of their interplay in Kingsolver's thick detail and high comic prose is among the glories of this novel.

The tragedy that triggers their exodus is the death of the youngest daughter, bitten by a snake that was planted by a shaman who has been antagonized equally, if oppositely, by her proselytizing father and gender-defying sister. Now finally the mother steps forward to lead her remaining daughters from the village and their father, and this journey ends with Rachel and Leah remaining in Africa when their mother and sister Adah return to the United States. Here I skip most of the novel to focus on these two during its last 150 pages, where they can illustrate both the overdeterminations of gender, race, and class that continue to govern the narrative and also now finally the form of the whole.

Rachel, the eldest, is a platinum blonde, beauty queen/cheerleader fastidious about her clothes, food, and hygiene. She disdains the Congo from day one, along with her father for bringing her there, and longs for the commodities she had to leave behind. But even without them she is a sexual magnet: the village chief chooses her to add to his household, and when she escapes this fate she marries another admirer, Eeben Axelroot, the barnstorming pilot with the shortwave radio secretly employed by the CIA. They move to South Africa, where he becomes a philandering diamond merchant and she leaves him for a social ascent through two more marriages that land her finally in French Congo as the widowed proprietress of an elegant hotel, The Equatorial, whose black staff under her close supervision caters to European businessmen renewing the rape of Africa.

Leah Price, unlike her sister, has always loved her father and craved his love and approval. She begins by sharing his desire to reach out to Africa and helping him cultivate his demonstration garden of Kentucky Wonder Beans. But this Electra comes very soon to reject her father as mentor and role model. After the family catastrophe she marries the schoolteacher, Anatole Ngemba, a Lumumba supporter who will now be in and out of prison for many years, during which they have three children and join other families in trying to maintain a communal farm within Mobutu's starvation economy. This becomes next to impossible, and at the end they are hoping to move to a precariously more friendly environment in Angola.

The purposes and feelings that unite and divide these sisters as white women living in Africa can be seen conveniently in two episodes, their experience of the 1974 Ali-Foreman championship prizefight in Zaire—the "Rumble in the Jungle" by which Mobutu won international respectability for his renamed country with its savage regime—and their reunion ten years later when their sister Adah comes to visit from the United States. The overdeterminations involved in these episodes are both thematic and rhetorical, and in this regard nothing could be more Dickensian in relation to its audience than Kingsolver's making Rachel the Cold War beauty queen her frequent and reliable narrator.

We know as historical fact that hundreds of political prisoners were shackled beneath the boxing ring before, during, and after the Ali-Foreman fight, and when Leah's Anatole is arrested and sent to prison, possibly for life, at the time of the fight, she is grateful that his incarceration will occur not beneath the boxing ring but in the far preferable prison where Lumumba was beaten half to death. Meanwhile, she says,

> People from the world over will come watch this great event, two black men knocking each other senseless for five million dollars apiece. And they'll go away never knowing that in all of goddamned Zaire not one public employee outside the goddamned army has been paid in two years. (451)

Rachel on the other hand experiences the prizefight as a missed opportunity for a family reunion:

> I will probably grow very rich and very old at The Equatorial before any member of my family ever visits me here. It's true! They never have. Leah is right over there in Kinshasa, which is just a hop, skip, and jump away. When they had that fight down there with Muhammad Ali and George Foreman we had *tons* of tourists from that . . . I knew we'd get a slew of people. I've always had a sixth sense for spotting a trend coming, and I was right on the ball. I finished up the second-floor bathroom I'd been having trouble with, and redecorated the bar with a boxing theme . . .
>
> I kept thinking, everyone is in such a festive mood, and Leah is not that far away, in miles. Mother and Adah keep saying they might come over to visit, and if they could cross an entire ocean, you would think Leah could stoop to taking a bus. (463)

Here is a sensibility and intonation out of Oprah Winfrey, yet you can no more condescend to Rachel Price than to *Little Dorrit*'s Flora Finching or John Chivery. Like them, she sometimes verges on caricature, but she is also endowed like them with a vitality, presence, and dignity that make her proof against satire and in fact qualify her for her role in telling the story.

We hear her again, ten years further on, when Leah herself arranges a family reunion while Anatole is again in prison. Their sister Adah crosses the ocean with a rebuilt Land Rover for the communal farm, and the three take a driving holiday during which Leah and Rachel argue nonstop about the communist threat to Africa. Here Rachel's enveloping narrative is far more engaging than Leah's predictable political analysis, yet in no way dilutes the force of that analysis, which Kingsolver clearly wants her reader to accept. Rachel's politics are all wrong, but she is really a hoot:

> Leah and Adah and I started bickering practically the minute we met up in Senegal. We could never even agree on where to go or stay or what to eat. Whenever we found any place that was just the teeniest step above horrid, Leah felt it was too expensive. She and Anatole evidently have chosen to live like paupers. And Adah, helpful as always, would chime in with a list of what disease organisms were likely to be present. We argued about everything: even communism! Which you would think there was nothing to argue about. I merely gave Leah the very sensible advice that she should think twice about going to Angola because the Marxists are taking it over.
>
> "The Mbundu and the Kongo tribes have a long-standing civil war there, Rachel. Agostinho Neto led the Mbundu to victory because he had the most popular support."
>
> "Well, for your information, Dr. Henry Kissinger himself says that Neto and them are followers of Karl Marx, and the other ones are pro-United States."
>
> "Imagine that," Leah said. "The Mbundu and Kongo people have been at war with each other for the last six hundred years, and Dr. Henry Kissinger has at last discovered the cause . . . "
>
> "Hah," Adah said. Her first actual unrehearsed syllable of the day. She talks now, but she still doesn't exactly throw words away.
>
> Adah was in the back, and Leah and me up front . . . I had to slow way down for a stop sign because the rivers in West Africa were turning out to be as bad as the ones in Brazzaville. It was very hard to concentrate while my sisters were giving me a pop quiz on world democracy. (477–8)

Later the conversation turns to their father, of whose death Leah has learned and now reports, but still within Rachel's narration. When a canoe with children overturned in the baptismal river and the crocodiles got at the children, the now grizzled, long-haired old man, who'd had nothing to do with this, was nevertheless held responsible and chased by the natives up an old wooden fire tower, to which they then set fire. As the only daughter who actually loved him, Leah begins crying as she tells the story, and Rachel says,

> I could see this was hard for Leah. I reached out and took hold of her hand. "Honey, I know," I told her. "He was our daddy. I think you always put up with him better than any of us. But he was mean as a snake. There's nothing he got that he didn't deserve."
>
> She pulled her hand out of mine so she could wipe her eyes and blow her nose. "I know that!" She sounded mad. (486)

Rachel's observation and tenderness are as much a part of her as her bourgeois Cold War smugness, and in her Dickensian presence, as in all three of her sisters', Kingsolver engages a popular audience in an overdetermined rhetoric inseparable from the overdeterminations of her story itself.

3

There is of course nothing new about an open-ended novel, and theorists regularly argue with Bakhtin that open-endedness belongs to the novel as a genre. But there are different situations, characters, actions, or themes to be open-ended *about*, and here I think some old distinctions can still be maintained among, for example, the picaresque novel, the novel of character (or *Bildung*), and what I want to call here the novel of history. Saul Bellow said somewhere something to the effect that when he's through with his heroes he just dumps them, and for my white male American generation Bellow's are the great examples of novelistic open-endedness. Augie March walking at the end on the Normandy beach, Henderson running breathlessly on the Newfoundland ice, or Herzog crashing in his new-old farmhouse, could have been dumped at many points along the way— or else saved for further adventures before returning home when they do. Narratologically withheld and shielded from the concrete overdeterminations of actual history, their monovocal, self-determined characters are Bellow's point of entry, and their adventures subsumed by that point of entry can begin or end at will. Historically speaking, they are always free to come home because their travels have been metaphorical and they never really left. In Bellow's great send-up of Hemingway, Henderson the Rain King in fact goes to Africa to check out his manhood. But his and Hemingway's Africa (like Conrad's) is light years away from the Prices' Africa, which has a history of its own to be engaged and negotiated. Theirs is instead a metaphorical Africa, a scene-painted backdrop for the hero's experience of struggle with himself.

By contrast, all five narrators of *The Poisonwood Bible* experience Africa as Davis's "conflicted subject[s] engaged in the effort to mediate historical contradiction through recourse to thought."[3] Their voices are as distinctive and engaging as those of Bellow's heroes, but they also experience themselves as caught up in irreversible historical processes to which they have no choice but to respond. Directly or indirectly, they know they must answer for the ways in which their personal histories are woven into the material process of a community bigger than they are, in which whatever choice you make, you can't go home again.

At any of several junctures Rachel Price could have returned to the United States for a putatively comic closure at the shopping mall and the beauty parlor. But she stays in Africa to run The Equatorial, "which isn't just a hotel, it's like running a whole little *country*" (512; emphasis in text), and here is how she explains at age 50 why she could never return:

> I had my bags packed more than once. But when push came to shove, I was always afraid. Of what? Well, it's hard to explain. Scared I wouldn't be able to fit back in is the long and short of it. I was only nineteen or twenty at that time. My high school friends would still have been whining over boyfriends and fighting for carhop jobs at the A&W. Their idea of a dog-eat-dog world was Beauty School. And now here comes Rachel with stained hair and one dead sister and a whole darn marriage behind her already . . .
>
> "What was it like over there?" I could just hear them asking. What would I say? "Well, the ants nearly ate us alive. Everybody we knew kept turning up dead of one disease and another. The babies all got diarrhea and plumb dried up. When we got hungry we'd go shoot animals and strip off their hides."
>
> Let's face it, I could never have been popular again at home. (512–13)

Leah and Anatole also could have returned rather than risk further poverty, malaria, and imprisonment, and at one point they explore that possibility. They come to the United States as graduate students at Emory, Leah in agricultural engineering and Anatole in political science, with teaching assistantships and student housing that make them wealthy by Congolese standards. But there are no smells in America; their trilingual children, who "fluently interchange French, Lingala, and English, with a slight accent in each," are spoken to by white Americans in "broad, loud baby talk"; and on the street these Americans scowl at their family for being

> the scourge they already knew and loathed—the mixed-race couple, with mongrel children as advertisement for our sins. Drawing nearer they would always stare at Anatole as contempt gave way to bald shock. His warrior's face with its expertly carved lines speaks its elegance in a language as foreign to them as Lingala. (468)

Leah decides that "I can't drag a husband and sons into a life where their beauty will blossom and wither in darkness," and "So we came home. Here [i.e., Zaire]. To disaster. Anatole's passport was confiscated at the airport" (469). Anatole is sent again to prison, and when he is released one more time, "with nothing else to hope for, we lean toward Angola, while the past grows heavy and our future narrows down to a crack in the door" (503).

That crack in the door is Kingsolver's equivalent to Dickens's "roaring streets" into which Amy Dorrit and Arthur Clennam, also with nothing else to hope for, must descend after their marriage. They and the Price sisters are the same recognizable, deep-structure personalities we knew at the beginning but now are changed forever by having mediated historical contradiction in the material living of their lives. The open-endedness of their stories is both rhetorical and historical: their crack in the door parallels the Zapatistas' and is also perfectly congruent with that of their popular audience—whether facing alienation in Dickens's London streets or complicity in capitalism's destruction of Kingsolver's African peoples. Where a Marxian imagination produces tragedy in the other writers I have discussed, in Dickens and Kingsolver it produces Marxian tragedy's Marxian alternative, not historical novels but novels of contingent history—the history their audience itself must transact when it must necessarily participate in the processes of class.

NOTES

CHAPTER 1

1 Lionel Trilling, *The Liberal Imagination* (New York: Viking, 1950), 298. Further references to this work will be indicated in the text.

2 I also conceive my analysis as both an extension and a qualification of the analysis developed by Barbara Foley in *Radical Representations: Politics and Form in U.S. Proletarian Fiction, 1929–1941* (Durham, N.C.: Duke University Press, 1993).

3 F. S. C. Northrop, *The Logic of the Sciences and Humanities* (Cleveland, Ohio: World Publishing Company, 1963), 35–58.

4 "*Ressentiment* is the primal class passion, and here begins to govern the relations between the living and the dead: for the step from envy to hatred is a short one, and if the truth were told, the ghosts we are able to see hate the living and wish them harm. Such would at least be the only materialist way of thinking about it" ("Marx's Purloined Letter," *New Left Review*, I: 209 [Jan.–Feb. 1995], 86).

5 Stephen A. Resnick and Richard P. Wolff, *Knowledge and Class* (Chicago: University of Chicago Press, 1987), 159. Further references to this work, abbreviated *KC*, will be indicated in the text.

6 Here I am indebted to an unpublished paper by Eric Schocket, "Problems in the Study of Working-Class Culture."

7 For example, by Judith Butler in *Gender Trouble* (New York: Routledge, 1990), David Roediger in *The Wages of Whiteness* (New York: Verso, 1991), and Eve Kosofsky Sedgwick in *Epistemology of the Closet* (Berkeley: University of California Press, 1990).

8 E. P. Thompson, "Eighteenth-Century English Society: Class Struggle without Class?," *Social History*, 3 (1978), 147. Further references to this work, abbreviated "Eighteenth-Century," will be indicated in the text.

9 E. P. Thompson, *The Making of the English Working Class* (New York: Pantheon, 1963), 10. Further references to this work, abbreviated *MEWC*, are indicated in the text. Although my understanding of Thompson finally differs from hers, it is deeply indebted to Ellen Meiksins Wood's exposition of his thought in *Democracy against Capitalism* (Cambridge: Cambridge University Press, 1995), especially ch. 3, "Class as Process and Relationship," pp. 76–107.

10 Erik Olin Wright, *Classes* (London: Verso, 1985), 19.

11 Louis Althusser, *For Marx* (London: Verso, 1990), 101; emphasis in text.

12 Stephen A. Resnick and Richard P. Wolff, "The New Marxian Political Economy and the Contribution of Althusser," *Postmodern Materialism and the Future of Marxist Theory*, ed. Antonio Callari and David F. Ruccio (Hanover, N.H.: University Press of New England, 1996), 174, 171.

13 Ellen Meiksins Wood, *The Retreat from Class: A New "True" Socialism* (London: Verso, 1986), 76; emphasis in text.

14 George Eliot, *Middlemarch* (Oxford: Oxford University Press, 1996), 132.

15 Might we not argue that if class itself disappears historically, as Marxism claims it eventually will, Marxism itself will also disappear—or at least forfeit any special claim to authority in defining the character of a classless society?

16 Perhaps it needs saying here that my imagination of class is not a Romantic imagination producing "organic" rather than "mechanical" form by seeing the world in a grain of sand. This imagination does not, in Coleridge's words, dissolve, diffuse, and dissipate in order to re-create. Instead it penetrates by abstraction the material overdeterminations by which class is mediated to our experience so as to see the material process in which class is organic to our experience. In this respect it is more like Coleridge's scientific imagination producing "mechanical" form by abstracting the cosmological or geological processes mediated in our experience of earthly or celestial harmonies and disruptions.

17 I do not think it an accident that contemporary academic leftists who bemoan the impotence of the left also share in the academy's condescension to realism as an obsolete and inferior fictional form. The realist novel is at very least a first step into the awareness of class as expropriation, and devoted readers of that novel have regularly been among the more precocious members of political movements striving to overcome the impotence of the left.

18 This is ultimately too simple a distinction. Fictional characters at a single identity site are still ideologically overdetermined and—as in a whole spectrum of Toni Morrison's characters—may identify with their class, race, or gender positions either willingly, conflictually, resistingly, or not at all. Yet however that may be, it is only the structure and progression of an entire novel that can retrieve class from the political unconscious and represent it both mimetically and conceptually as a historical process of expropriation.

19 *The Dollmaker* was runner-up to Faulkner's *The Fable* for the 1954 National Book Award, and in Erica Jong's 1998 women's alternative list (produced by an informal e-mail poll) to the Modern Library's proclaimed 100 best novels of the twentieth century, it came in thirteenth, after four by Virginia Woolf and three by Edith Wharton in the dozen ahead of it. See Jong, "I've Got a Little List," *The Nation*, 16 Nov. 1998, 32–35.

20 Joyce Carol Oates, Afterword to *The Dollmaker*, by Harriet Arnow (New York: Avon Books, 1989), 601, 607, 608.

21 Harriet Arnow, *The Dollmaker* (New York: Avon Books, 1989), 318. Further references to this work will be indicated in the text.

22 Kathleen R. Parker, "American Migration Pattern in Exaggerated Relief," *Harriet Simpson Arnow: Critical Essays on Her Work*, ed. Haeja K. Chung (East Lansing, Mich.: Michigan State University Press, 1995), 213.

23 Here and in what follows I am deeply indebted to Ellen Meiksins Wood, *The Pristine Culture of Capitalism* (New York: Verso, 1991).

24 I develop this analysis of the play at greater length in "Shakespeare's Materialism in *King Lear*," *Rethinking Marxism*, vol. 4, no. 3 (1991), 101–108, and in *Melville and the Politics of Identity: From King Lear to Moby-Dick* (Champaign, Ill.: University of Illinois Press, 1993). My argument is that Edgar survives long enough to vanquish Edmund only by abandoning Cordelia's feudal ethics and embracing Edmund's capitalist ethics, and then by applying those ethics opportunistically—in the only way possible—on behalf of a conception of justice that is systemically alien to capitalism.

CHAPTER 2

1 George Bernard Shaw, *Shaw on Dickens*, ed. Dan H. Laurence and Martin Quinn (New York: Frederick Ungar, 1985), 27. Further references to this work will be indicated in the text.

2 B. H. Haggin, *The Listener's Musical Companion* (New York: Oxford, 1991), 59.

3 The pioneer Marxist study of Dickens is T. A. Jackson, *Charles Dickens: The Progress of a Radical* (London: Lawrence & Wishart, 1937). Even more useful for the approach I develop here, in its implicit reliance on a theory of overdetermined social processes, is James M. Brown, *Dickens: Novelist in the Market-Place* (Totowa, N.J.: Barnes & Noble, 1982). On the other hand, Pam Morris, in *Dickens's Class Consciousness: A Marginal View* (London: Macmillan, 1991), relies almost entirely on the conception of class as an identity site.

Myron Magnet, in *Dickens and the Social Order*, exhibits in detail the "conservative view with which his [Dickens's] liberal reformism is inextricably intertwined" and shows how *Nicholas Nickleby*, *Barnaby Rudge*, and *Martin Chuzzlewit* reflect an essentially Hobbesian conception of human aggressiveness and the consequent need for a Leviathanic social order. Magnet's argument that for all Dickens's hijinks, sentimentality, and philistinism, he "is nevertheless a novelist who *thinks*" (Myron Magnet, *Dickens and the Social Order* [Philadelphia: University of Pennsylvania Press, 1985], 8, 71; emphasis in text), along with his argument that the combined achievement of these earlier novels would have made Dickens a major novelist even if he had written no more, suggests all the more an element of inexorability in Dickens's gravitation, as a novelist who thinks, toward the political and social novel.

4 Charles Dickens, *Hard Times*, The Oxford Illustrated Dickens (Oxford: Oxford University Press, 1955), 63. Further references to this work will be indicated in the text.

5 Dickens's letters, speeches, and journalism are consistent in affirming that, as he put it in an 1853 speech to the Birmingham workers, "the welfare of society" consists "in the fusion of different classes, without confusion; in the bringing together of employers and employed; in the creating of a better common understanding among those whose interests are identical, who depend upon each other, and who can never be in unnatural antagonism without deplorable results" (quoted in *Hard Times: A Norton Critical Edition*, third edition, ed. Fred Kaplan and Sylvère Monod [New York: Norton, 2001], 278). For and illumination of Dickens's views

on class, see Trey Philpots, "'To Working Men' and 'The People': Dickens's View of Class Relations in the Months Preceding *Little Dorrit*," *Dickens Quarterly* 7:2 (1990), 262–74.

6 It can be argued that Dickens's view of the workers as deluded is consistent with his view that the classes have common interests and need each other: the workers' delusions reflect an incorrigible ignorance that must be corrected by the (potentially) more enlightened views of the employers. But Blackpool's speech to Bounderby, which Dickens's narrative clearly endorses, can also be read to argue precisely the opposite—that the workers are fully capable of thinking for themselves—so that Dickens's muddle remains in any case and he has to kill off Blackpool for being too uppity.

7 Philip Hobsbaum, *A Reader's Guide to Charles Dickens* (London: Thames and Hudson, 1972), 183–4.

8 Patricia E. Johnson, "*Hard Times* and the Structure of Industrialism: The Novel as Factory," *Hard Times: A Norton Critical Edition*, ed. Fred Kaplan and Sylvère Monod (New York: Norton, 2001), 418. Further references to this essay will be indicated in the text.

9 Terry Eagleton, *Criticism and Ideology* (London: New Left Books, 1976), 129; emphasis in text.

10 Charles Dickens, *Our Mutual Friend* (Oxford: Oxford University Press, 1952), 821.

11 Charles Dickens, *Little Dorrit* (Oxford: Oxford University Press, 1953), 711. Further references to this work will be indicated in the text.

12 Cf. H. Ross Dabney:

> It [*Little Dorrit*] is much less concerned with the miseries of the poor than either *Hard Times* or *Bleak House*. Although logically we must expect the tenants of Bleeding Heart Yard to suffer from the defects of their governors and of the political and economic systems these governors maintain, we do not in fact see them suffer very much. Dickens enforces a vision of pride of place, self-will, inertia, anxiety, and concealment as dominating motives in the governing and propertied classes of his civilization; he is essentially concerned with the moral implications of these motives rather than the economic and political effects on the community. (Ross H. Dabney, *Love and Property in the Novels of Dickens* [Berkeley: University of California Press, 1967], 95–6)

But I will argue that Dickens's concern with "the moral implications of these motives" is constituted by his parallel concerns with the sanctity of labor and the moral devastation entailed by the appropriation of surplus labor.

13 Harriet Beecher Stowe, *Uncle Tom's Cabin* (New York: Random House, 1938), 291; emphasis in text.

14 Stephen Jay Gould, *Ever Since Darwin* (New York: Norton, 1997).

15 George Lukács, *Studies in European Realism* (New York: Grosset and Dunlap, 1964), 61; emphasis in text.

16 I first saw this alleged statement of Shaw's in Lionel Trilling's Introduction to the Oxford Illustrated *Little Dorrit*. But it is nowhere to be found in *Shaw on Dickens*, a comprehensive compilation of Shaw's writing on Dickens. What Shaw does say is that

> One of the greatest books in the English language is *Little Dorrit*, and when the English nation realizes it is a great book and a true book there will be a revolution in this country. One of the reasons I am a revolutionist is that I read *Little Dorrit* when I was a little boy. (111)

He also says several times that what he and Sidney Webb have in common is their boyhood reading of *Little Dorrit*, which he describes as a "more seditious book than *Das Kapital*" (51).

17 "Citizen," like "humanism," has become a contested word and concept, in this case through its association with the patriarchal tradition of the Enlightenment. But while I don't think this term is irreplaceable, I do not see how we can do without any terminology for the public space and personal status in which to seek common ground for our many identities. Those devoted to identity politics often recognize that somewhere along the line it may become important to pursue what they call "coalition politics." But on which turf will coalitions be formed, and what will become the identities of those who sustain their coalitions?

CHAPTER 3

1 Honoré de Balzac, author's Introduction, *The Human Comedy*, 3 vols. (New York: F. P. Collier, 1893), 1: lvi–lvii.

2 David Lodge, *The Modes of Modern Writing* (Ithaca, N.Y.: Cornell University Press, 1977), 25.

3 "Their [Balzac's and James's] realistic intentions naturally lead them to describe and analyse systems of behavior, communication, exploitation, and so on, that structure the world, and to rely . . . upon these systems to help structure their texts and to provide them with figurative language" (William W. Stowe, *Balzac, James, and the Realist Novel* [Princeton: Princeton University Press, 1983], 8). Other useful analyses of realism, rhetorical and historical, are George Becker, Introduction, *Documents of Modern Literary Realism*, ed. George Becker (Princeton: Princeton University Press, 1963) and George Levine, *The Realist Imagination* (Chicago: University of Chicago Press, 1981).

4 Even so, the unmistakable prominence of class in *Tar Baby* may be what has made it less inviting to academic attention than Morrison's other novels.

5 Lukács's realism can be seen as his alternative to reification where literary representation is concerned. J. M. Bernstein argues that, for Lukács, "pre-capitalist epic narratives were structured by value-systems and beliefs whose validity was authenticated by the practices and institutions of society at large" and that the reified world of capitalism is "no longer value-oriented and structured in this way," so that the novel, unlike the epic, "must represent the objective world as devoid of value" and then create value through its own "dialectic of form-giving and mimesis" (J. M. Bernstein, *The Philosophy of the Novel: Lukács, Marxism and the Dialectics of Form* [Brighton, U.K.: Harvester Press, 1984], xvii). In such a dialectic, it can then be argued, literary mimesis is constantly vulnerable to being reified in forms such as

naturalism and expressionism, against both of which Lukács waged a lifelong polemic.

6 "'Tendency' or Partisanship?," *Essays in Realism*, by George Lukács, ed. Rodney Livingstone (Cambridge, Mass.: MIT Press, 1981), 41. Further references to this work, abbreviated "Tendency," will be indicated in the text.

7 George Lukács, "Tolstoy and the Development of Realism," *Studies in European Realism* (New York: Grosset and Dunlap, 1964), 147. Further references to this work, abbreviated "Tolstoy," will be indicated in the text.

8 Like *Tar Baby*, *Little Dorrit* seems to have less credibility among academics than its author's other novels, and that could be because its production of class as point of entry is so hard to ignore.

9 Henry James, *The Princess Casamassima*, 2 vols. (New York: Scribners, 1907), 1: 141. Further references to this work will be indicated in the text.

10 James could have been aware that during the Paris Commune some of the Communards vandalized public buildings and defaced works of art. See Rupert Christiansen, *Paris Babylon* (New York: Viking, 1995), 334–54.

11 Henry Roth, *Shifting Landscape* (New York: St. Martin's, 1987), 47.

12 The complex relations of rhetoric and style to a narratology of overdetermination would have to be the subject of a chapter in itself. I can only say here that while the realist novel is fundamentally devoted to "literal" representation, it also includes metaphoric forms of cognition. It is both documentary and symbolic, and solely in its documentary function it is not always equipped to represent convincingly the processes of overdetermination.

13 Mary Heaton Vorse, *Strike!* (New York: Liveright, 1930), 270.

14 Fielding Burke, *Call Home the Heart* (Old Westbury, Conn.: The Feminist Press, 1983), 306.

15 "People who've lived through a great, great thing like that strike of 1937, people who called each other brother and sister and meant it, people who would give things to other families' kids because it was needed—when you saw that kind of loyalty to a person in the same boat as you, you can never forget, and I hope that feeling will come back some day." (Genora Johnson Dollinger, quoted in Studs Terkel, *Coming of Age* [New York: The New Press, 1995], 104.)

16 Here a distinction can be made between the experience of class consciousness and the experience of classlessness. In both strikes and strike novels workers find solidarity in their mutual awareness of their conditions of expropriation—a Thompsonian, consciousness-raising awareness of themselves as a class in opposition to another class. This is perhaps what Lukács had in mind as "the consciousness of the proletariat" freeing itself from reification. Then on occasion, as in episodes where the better-off strikers share their homes or food with their worse-off comrades, this immediate class unity produces intimations of a classless community where the rule is "from each according to her ability, to each according to her need."

17 Alexander Saxton, *The Great Midland* (Champaign, Ill.:University of Illinois Press, 1987), 135–6. Further references to this work will be indicated in the text.

18 Constance Coiner and Alan Wald, the two scholars to whom we owe *The Great Midland*'s republication, both write as if the novel's signal success were its portrait of Stephanie. Coin-

er describes her excitement in discovering the novel partly as follows: "I puzzled over how a fiction writer—especially a *male* writer—could have produced a female character such as Stephanie Koviak . . . before feminism's second wave" (Constance Coiner, "The Old Left and Cross-Gendered Writing", in *The Great Midland*, by Alexander Saxton [Champaign, Ill.: University of Illinois Press, 1997], xii; emphasis in text). Wald describes Stephanie as the novel's "major site of internalized ideological struggle between middle- and working-class pressures" (Alan Wald, *Writing from the Left* [London: Verso, 1994], 188).

19 In *Little Dorrit* Dickens interweaves from beginning to end his multiple stories involving religion, imprisonment, labor, and class, and this gives class as point of entry in its many overdeterminations a compelling rhetorical power.

20 Meridel Le Sueur, *The Girl* (Minneapolis: West End Press, 1978), 125. Further references to this work will be indicated in the text.

21 Rabinowitz claims that in the classic proletarian novel, history and class consciousness are gendered as masculine, and desire as feminine. She then argues that *The Girl* is a) "a narrative of female desire in which maternal power is processed through heterosexuality," thereby enabling women to become historical subjects, and b) a narrative "that verges on essentialism because it invokes women's biological capacity to bear children without interrogating the cultural platitudes surrounding motherhood" (Paula Rabinowitz, *Labor and Desire* [Chapel Hill: University of North Carolina Press, 1991], 123). Coiner essentially agrees: "To the extent that *The Girl* promotes biologism, binary logic, and woman as myth, the novel supports the very system it seeks to destroy" (Constance Coiner, *Better Red: The Writing and Resistance of Tillie Olsen and Meridel Le Sueur* [New York: Oxford University Press, 1995], 121).

CHAPTER 4

1 Aijaz Ahmad, *In Theory* (London: Verso, 1992), 92.

2 Henry James, *The Princess Casamassima,* 2 vols. (New York: Scribners, 1908), 1:141. Further references to this work will be indicated in the text.

3 Ellen Meiksins Wood, *The Retreat from Class: A New "True" Socialism* (London: Verso, 1998).

4 *The Notebooks of Henry James*, ed. F. O. Matthiessen and Kenneth Murdock (New York: Oxford University Press, 1947), 68.

5 James describes his effort in the Preface as follows:

> Face to face with the idea of Hyacinth's subterraneous politics and occult affiliations, I recollect perfectly feeling . . . that I might well be ashamed if, with my advantages—and there wasn't a street, a corner, an hour of London that wasn't an advantage—I shouldn't be able to piece together a proper semblance of those things. . . . (I: xxii)

6 *Henry James Letters*, 4 vols., ed. Leon Edel (Cambridge, Mass.: Harvard University Press, 1974–84), 3: 64. Further references to this work will be indicated in the text.

7 The regularity with which bourgeois apologists have made this claim, along with the falsity of the claim, have been documented by the British Marxist "historians from below," especially George Rudé in *The French Revolution* (New York: Grove Press, 1988) and *Ideology and Popular Protest* (Chapel Hill: University of North Carolina Press, 1995) , and E. P. Thompson in *The Making of the English Working Class* (New York: Random House, 1966) and *Customs in Common* (New York: The New Press, 1993).

8 Henry James, "The Art of Fiction," *Essays on Literature: American Writers; English Writers*, ed. Leon Edel (New York: Library of America, 1984), 46.

9 The four chapters devoted to Medley total 80 pages, in which it's as if James's intensity of feeling and stylistic appetite can't get enough of his subject in depicting Hyacinth's impressions of the park and gardens, the interior of the house, the rhythm of the meals, the Princess playing the piano, the Princess's conversation. Hyacinth's European tour, on the other hand, takes two chapters amounting to 27 pages, and, except for his five-page letter to the Princess from Venice, these pages record his reflections on his friends back home rather than his impressions of Europe.

10 It has been argued that *The Princess* represents nineteenth-century anarchism rather than socialism, and in respect to its assassination plot that may be true. But there were varieties of anarchism just as of socialism, and I think it is clear that James conceived his radical movement so as to include its specifically socialist aspirations.

11. Fyodor Dostoevsky, *Diary of a Writer*, trans. Boris Brasol (Santa Barbara, Cal.: Peregrine Smith, 1979), 142–154.

12 Fyodor Dostoevsky, *Demons*, trans. Richard Pevear and Larissa Volkhovonsky (New York: Knopf, 1994), 392.

13 These two passages constitute a knowing abstract of Dickens's depiction of exploitation and misery from *Oliver Twist* to *Little Dorrit*, and it's as if James knew himself better than to attempt Dickens's concrete representation even as he tried to borrow some of Dickens's rhetorical power. Similarly, Lady Aurora's work among the poor gave James the opportunity for scenes like those in *Bleak House* where Esther and Ada visit the bricklayers' battered wives, and this too he declined.

14 Seeing her this way would also make plausible James's claim in the Preface that he had not finished with Christina Light in *Roderick Hudson* and could now happily recall her in the character of the Princess. Recalling her as a *capricciosa* is not to finish with her but simply to recycle her.

15 Just as Hyacinth is steeped in London, London is steeped in Dickensian fog. But James's fog differs from *Bleak House*'s fog in its tragic ambiguity. Sometimes it "blurred and suffused the whole place . . . produced halos and dim radiations" (1: 82), and sometimes "the silent vista of the street . . . stretched away in the wintry drizzle to right and left, losing itself in the huge tragic city where unmeasured misery lurked beneath the dirty night" (1:358). And when the fog finally lifts on the night Hyacinth receives his summons, "there was nothing to look at but the vista of low black houses, the dim inter-spaced street lamps, the prowling cats . . . and the terrible mysterious far off stars, which appeared to him more

than ever to see everything of our helplessness and tell nothing of help" (2:374).

16 Jeffrey Vogel, "The Tragedy of History," *New Left Review*, 220 (1996), 36. Further references to this work will be indicated in the text.

17 "If Rawls is to provide an account of history compatible with his moral theory then he must also explain why the alternative, morally desirable paths of development were not actually followed, and give reasons for these failures, other than non-explanations like human perfidy, selfishness or unwillingness to follow the correct principles of justice . . . Mill will face similar difficulties" (53).

18 Alan Wald, *The New York Intellectuals* (Chapel Hill, N.C.: University of North Carolina Press, 1987). Wald devotes a section of a chapter to Lionel Trilling on pp. 33–36 and another to Irving Howe on pp. 311–20.

19 For example, Alexander Saxton, the novelist and historian. In a reminiscence of party membership in his 1997 Introduction to the reprint of his novel *The Great Midland* (Champaign, Ill.: University of Illinois Press, 1997), Saxton says,

> If my claim to historical accuracy has any validity, it tends to negate the theory of American Communism as a conspiracy by party bureaucrats in New York to gain power and prestige by serving as running dogs of a foreign power. The neighborhood and industrial branches I knew in Chicago linked into sequences that ran separately from national leadership. (xviii)

That was also my experience in Chicago, which may call into question the New York intellectuals' monolithic version of CP political and cultural debate based on their experience east of the Hudson River. For a version very different from theirs, which shows some number of party intellectuals engaging the complex relations between literature and politics with a sophistication matching theirs, see Barbara Foley, *Radical Representations: Politics and Form in U.S. Proletarian Fiction, 1929–1941* (Durham, N.C.: Duke University Press, 1993) and James Murphy, *The Proletarian Moment* (Champaign, Ill.: University of Illinois Press, 1991).

20 "It is very difficult to be certain about Trilling's politics in the thirties because he left few traces. But it appears, from his writing and associations, that he was involved with revolutionary Marxist thinking for at least two or three years after quitting the Communist-controlled NCDPP in 1933. Altogether, Trilling's adherence to revolutionary politics probably lasted about four years" (Mark Krupnick, *Lionel Trilling and the Fate of Cultural Criticism* [Evanston, Ill.: Northwestern University Press, 1986], 40). See also Diana Trilling, *The Beginning of the Journey* (New York: Harcourt Brace, 1993), 193–218.

21 Lionel Trilling, "*The Princess Casamassima*," *The Liberal Imagination* (New York: Viking, 1950), 80. Further references to this work will be indicated in the text.

22 It was also a commonplace among New York intellectuals that their contemporaries who remained members of the Communist Party did so only for psychological reasons. Like Trilling's Hyacinth tempted to escape from isolation, they were lonely and frustrated people seeking identity and fulfillment in a cause.

23 Irving Howe, "Henry James: The Political Vocation," in *Politics and the Novel* (New York: Horizon Publishers, 1957), 141. Further references to this work will be indicated in the text.

24 Irving Howe, *The Radical Papers* (New York: Doubleday, 1966), 3. Howe wrote book-length polemical histories—of the United Auto Workers (with B. J. Widick), the CPUSA (with Lewis Coser), and socialism in America. But nowhere that I know of does he directly engage class as a historical process independent of political movements.

25 Both Trilling's and Howe's essays are divided into subsections devoted to aspects of *The Princess* that are not only unrelated but sometimes contradictory—as when Trilling devotes one subsection to Hyacinth as a child in an adult world, which effectively disqualifies him for the tragic role Trilling has claimed for him in an earlier section.

26 Mark Seltzer, "*The Princess Casamassima*: Realism and the Fantasy of Surveillance," in *Henry James and the Art of Power* (Ithaca, N.Y.: Cornell University Press, 1984).

CHAPTER 5

1. Antonio Gramsci, *Selections from the Prison Notebooks*, ed. Quintin Hoare and Geoffrey Nowell-Smith (New York: International Publishers, 1971), 12. Further references to this work will be indicated in the text.

2 Gramsci later explains as follows the failure of Italy's "Popular Universities" devoted to adult education: "They could only have had cultural stability and an organic quality of thought if there had existed the same unity between the intellectuals and the simple as there should be between theory and practice. That is, if the intellectuals had been organically the intellectuals of those masses, and if they had worked out and made coherent the principles and problems raised by the masses in their practical activity, thus constituting a cultural and social bloc" (330).

3 Elaine Hedges, Introduction, *Ripening*, by Meridel Le Sueur, ed. Elaine Hedges (New York: the Feminist Press, 1990), 6; further references to this work, abbreviated "Hedges," will be indicated in the text. Linda Ray Pratt, Afterword, *I Hear Men Talking*, by Meridel Le Sueur (Minneapolis: West End Press, 1984), 227; further references to this work, abbreviated "Pratt," will be indicated in the text.

4 Howard Zinn, *A People's History of the United States* (New York: Harper, 1995), 332.

5 Meridel Le Sueur, *Crusaders* (St. Paul, Minn.: Minnesota Historical Society, 1984), xvi. Further references to this work, abbreviated *C*, will be indicated in the text.

6 Constance Coiner, *Better Red: The Writing and Resistance of Tillie Olsen and Meridel Le Sueur* (New York: Oxford University Press, 1995), 76–7. Further references to this work, abbreviated "Coiner," will be indicated in the text.

7 She also wrote a series of children's books for Alfred A. Knopf: *Little Brother of the Wilderness: The Story of Johnny Appleseed* (1947); *Nancy Hanks of Wilderness Road* (1949); *Sparrow Hawk* (1950); *Chanticleer of Wilderness Road* (1951); and *The River Road: A Story of Abraham Lincoln* (1954).

8 "For many people like Algren, Wright, and the feminist writer Meridel Le Sueur, the hope and support offered by the movement were succor to be found nowhere else. 'I don't think any of us would have survived without the Reed clubs and our bond with each other,' Le Sueur recalled . . . Still, it was not easy. 'It was a very hard time to live to be a writer,' she wrote. 'The left was very severe on you. It had its own orthodoxy . . . But it also summoned us forth . . . We wouldn't have tried without them . . . the Communists gave us light and even love'" (Bettina Drew, *Nelson Algren: A Life on the Wild Side* [New York: Putnam, 1989], 77).

9 Alan Wald, "The Many Lives of Meridel Le Sueur," *Monthly Review*, 49.4 (1997), 23.

10 Meridel Le Sueur, "The Fetish of Being Outside," *Harvest Song*, revised ed. (Albuquerque, N.M.: West End Press, 1990), 201. Further references to this work will be indicated in the text.

11 Le Sueur also cultivated direct contact with the people to whom she wanted to give voice. Beginning in the thirties, at different times she lived communally, sometimes by choice and sometimes because of her own poverty, with farm and proletarian women or on Native American reservations, and a number of her stories and essays involve bus trips whose purpose seems to have been concrete immersion in the world of the masses. (See Hedges, 9, 17–18.)

12 "It was not so simple as saying you are joining the working class," she said years later to Linda Ray Pratt. "You have to destroy the images. The problem is how to make this new image. To find the image of the oppressed instead of the oppressor is a violent, difficult thing" (Pratt, 229).

13 Le Sueur kept journals all her life, and Elaine Hedges wrote in 1982 that her journals then numbered "over 149 volumes" (Hedges, 23). These must contain as much writing as all her published work, and some of that seems likely to be further Gramscian polemic.

14 Meridel Le Sueur, "Persephone," *Ripening*, 78. Further references to this work will be indicated in the text.

15. In Stravinsky's haunting *Persephone* of 1934, set to a text by André Gide, these traditional intellectuals altered the myth initially by making Persephone descend to Hades of her own accord, out of compassion for the souls in torment there. But then they proceeded to a traditional "Part Three: Persephone Reborn," which begins with "And so, Homer tells us / Did Demophoon / Return Persephone to her mother / And to earth her spring." Le Sueur deforms the myth by problematizing this return, and thereby sets the agenda for much of her subsequent writing.

16 Meridel Le Sueur, "Corn Village," *Salute to Spring* (New York: International Publishers, 1940), 10. Further references to this work will be indicated in the text.

17 "I now question the lyricism of my earlier stories, as if they were covering the horror and the loss, the terrible sewage of bourgeois life" (Meridel Le Sueur, Afterword, *I Hear Men Talking* [Minneapolis: West End Press, 1984], 242). Further references to this work, abbreviated "Afterword," will be indicated in the text.

18 Meridel Le Sueur, "Tonight Is Part of the Struggle," *Salute to Spring* (New York: International Publishers, 1940), 125.

19 Meridel Le Sueur, "I Was Marching," *Ripening*, 160. Further references to this work will be indicated in the text.

20 An earlier paragraph in "I Was Marching" reads as follows:

> The truth is I was afraid. Not of the physical danger at all, but an awful fright of mixing, of losing myself, of being unknown and lost. I felt inferior. I felt no one would know me there, that all I had been trained to excel in would go unnoticed. I can't describe what I felt, but perhaps it will come near it to say that I felt I excelled in competing with others and I knew instantly that these people were not competing at all, that they were acting in a strange, powerful trance of movement *together*. And I was filled with longing to act with them and with fear that I could not. I felt I was borne out of every kind of life, thrown up alone, looking at other lonely people, a condition I had been in the habit of defending with various attitudes of cynicism, preciosity, defiance, and hatred. (158–9)

21 Meridel Le Sueur, "Women on the Breadlines," *Ripening*, 138. Further references to this work will be indicated in the text.

22 A key "transitional" story in this regard is "Biography of My Daughter," where the narrator and her daughters Rachel and Deborah, along with an unemployed mill worker friend, go to a tuberculosis sanitarium to visit another friend, one of those women who "never say anything for themselves" (*Ripening*, 98). Rhoda had worked her way through college, where she trained as a librarian, but could not find a library job and worked as a maid, a cook, and a waitress before going on relief and being diagnosed with tuberculosis. She has died before they arrive, and the narrator introduces this story by saying, "Rhoda has been buried two weeks now, and I really wrote this story tearing it out between my teeth when we were driving back from the sanitarium that morning when the corn was just ripening in the fields" (100). She goes on to explain how she has adopted Rhoda as her own daughter by the action of telling this story.

23 Meridel Le Sueur, "Sequel to Love," *Writing Red: An Anthology of American Women Writers, 1930–1940*, ed. Charlotte Nekola and Paula Rabinowitz (New York: The Feminist Press, 1987), 36.

24 Meridel Le Sueur, *I Hear Men Talking* (Minneapolis: West End Press, 1984), 129–30. Further references to this work will be indicated in the text.

25 Meridel Le Sueur, *The Girl* (Minneapolis, Minn.: West End Press, 1978), 125. Further references to this work will be indicated in the text.

26 John Crawford's Afterword to *The Dread Road* (Albuquerque: West End Press, 1991), 49–54, gives a full account of its gestation. Elaine Hedges describes the gestation and purport of "The Origins of Corn" in *Ripening*, 251–2.

27 Meridel Le Sueur, "The Origins of Corn," *Ripening*, 254.

28 The frontispiece photograph of *Ripening*, taken circa 1946, is of Le Sueur standing alone in a cornfield.

29 Meridel Le Sueur, *The Dread Road* (Albuquerque: West End Press, 1991), 47. *The Dread Road* is also a formal experiment in non-linear narrative, printed in three columns apparently intended to be read simultaneously. The wider central column is the narrative itself. The right-hand column is the narrator's intermittent stream-of-consciousness response to

her center-column narration, and the left-hand column is a series of quotations from Poe, whom she chose, Le Sueur says in her Author's Note, because "he reflected the dread road of his time and the continuing, hidden buried death in America" (61).

30 Quoted in John Ross, *Rebellion from the Roots: Indian Uprising in Chiapas* (Monroe, Maine: Common Courage Press, 1995), 4.

31 In appropriating Gramsci's thought for identity politics, postmodernism, and "post-Marxism," many of his interpreters ignore the interrelatedness of these distinctions. In so doing, they strip from his theory of hegemony its historicism of class, and theorize in its place what Ellen Meiksins Wood calls "the autonomization of ideology and politics" (*The Retreat from Class: A New 'True' Socialism* [London: Verso, 1986], 47). See, e.g., Renate Holub, *Antonio Gramsci: Beyond Marxism and Postmodernism* (London: Routledge, 1992) and Chantal Mouffe, *Gramsci and Marxist Theory* (London: Routledge, 1979).

32 A much-discussed recent refinement of theory, and an alternative to both Lenin and Gramsci, has been proposed by Michael Hardt and Antonio Negri in *Empire* (Cambridge, Mass.: Harvard University Press, 2000). Hardt and Negri argue that in our age of globalization, traditional working classes, political parties, and nation-states have been superseded as historical subjects by what they call "the multitude," which they describe as "a *new proletariat* and not a *new industrial working class*" (402; emphasis in text). This multitude is endowed with the universal human right to a social wage that would put an end to capitalist expropriation, and the right to this wage can be asserted successfully against international capitalism only through international networks that bypass the class and party politics of nation-states. In the new global capitalist circumstances as characterized by *Empire*, theorists like Lenin and Gramsci become irrelevant along with the nation-state whose politics they theorized.

CHAPTER 6

1 Both Williams and Jameson have been highly prolific, and I cannot attempt here a comprehensive critique of their work. Yet both are consistent enough in assumptions and practice to make possible a representative sampling, and I will focus on Williams's *Culture and Society* (1958), *The Long Revolution* (1961), and *Marxism and Literature* (1977), and on Jameson's *Marxism and Form* (1971), *The Political Unconscious* (1981), and "Postmodernism, or, The Cultural Logic of Late Capitalism" (1984), with some occasional glances at other works.

2 Raymond Williams, *Culture and Society: 1780–1950* (New York: Columbia University Press, 1958), xvii–xviii.

3 Raymond Williams, *Marxism and Literature* (Oxford: Oxford University Press, 1977), 19. Further references to this work, abbreviated *ML*, will be indicated in the text.

4 Raymond Williams, "Literature and Sociology," *Problems in Materialism and Culture* (London: Verso, 1980), 20.

5 Raymond Williams, *The Long Revolution* (New York: Columbia University Press, 1961), 48. Further references to this work, abbreviated *LR*, will be indicated in the text.

6 Here a question might be raised as to the coexistence of multiple structures of feeling, where communication depends on each one singly, in a hegemonic culture that is also said to produce a single sense of absolute because experienced reality. But I understand Williams to mean that hegemonic culture must still be a battleground among structures of feeling, each with its own "discourse community," and contemporary scholarship has shown again and again how this may be so.

7 Meridel Le Sueur, *Crusaders* (St. Paul: Minnesota Historical Society, 1984), xxi–xxii.

3. Stravinsky's oft-quoted statement, that "Very little immediate tradition lies behind *Le Sacre du Printemps*. I had only my ear to help me. I heard and wrote what I heard," is routinely modified by his critics who show in detail how *Le Sacre* was enabled in fact to jump ahead of its time by the prior material practice of *The Firebird* and *Zvezdoliki*.

9 It finally seems that what Williams means by art that reaches beyond its time and occasion is simply art that documents a progression among structures of feeling and, in so doing, can inspire future Marxists and interest future historians, as in the following passage from "Literature and Sociology":

> And what seems to me especially important in these changing structures of feeling is that they often precede those more recognizable changes of formal idea and belief which make up the ordinary history of consciousness, and that while they correspond very closely to a real social history, of men living in actual and changing social relations, they again often precede the more recognizable changes of formal institution and relationship, which are the more accessible, indeed the more normal, history. (25)

10 Raymond Williams, *The English Novel from Dickens to Lawrence* (New York: Oxford University Press, 1970), 9 passim. Further references to this work, abbreviated *EN*, will be indicated in the text.

11 Williams's contribution to cultural studies is often characterized as "culturalist" rather than "structuralist," for example, by Stuart Hall in "Cultural Studies: Two Paradigms," *Culture, Ideology, and Social Process: A Reader*, ed. Tony Bennett, et al., (London: Batsford, 1981), 19–37. But if I am right about Williams's claim that structures of feeling interlock in tension by way of "connecting characteristics" while also functioning to connect ideologies, he can also be seen as participating in the Marxian structuralisms derived from Lévi-Strauss.

12 Fredric Jameson, *The Political Unconscious: Narrative as a Socially Symbolic Act* (Ithaca, N.Y.: Cornell University Press, 1981), 102. Further references to this work, abbreviated *PU*, will be indicated in the text.

13 Although the following critique by Bruce Norton is directed specifically at Jameson's work on postmodernism, I will try to show how it applies to all of Jameson's work:

> Whatever the specificities of the Lukacsian and critical theory traditions within which Jameson first found his epochal footing, when he takes Mandel's "late capitalism" as the context for his work he embraces a proudly essentialist tradition devoted to demonstrating that capitalism has a *telos*. Marxism is thought to posit that as capital-

ism develops, this telos, enforced by the essential contradiction between the forces and relations of production, has its way. Capitalism must therefore be construed in a way that allows that to happen: It has to be an expressive totality—a system structured and driven by an abstractly fixed logic. (Bruce Norton, "Late Capitalism and Postmodernism: Jameson/Mandel," in *Marxism and the Postmodern Age*, ed. Antonio Callari, Stephen Cullenberg, and Carole Biewener [New York: Guilford, 1995], 65)

14 Walter A. Davis, *Inwardness and Existence* (Madison, Wis.: University of Wisconsin Press, 1989), 399, n. 23. Davis uses the term "dialectical pluralism" only in this footnote, but he explicates the concept throughout Ch. 5, especially pp. 322–4 and 342–6. Further references to this work will be indicated in the text.

15 Fredric Jameson, *Marxism and Form* (Princeton: Princeton University Press, 1971), 331. Further references to this work, abbreviated *MF*, will be indicated in the text.

17 Fredric Jameson, "Third World Literature in the Era of Multinational Capital," *Social Text* 15 (Fall 1986), 65–88. Aijaz Ahmad begins his critique of Jameson's "cognitive aesthetics" by confessing his awkwardness at criticizing a theorist whose work he has admired for many years (Aijaz Ahmad, *In Theory* [London: Verso, 1992], 95–6). But it seems to me that Ahmad's critique applies as well to these other phrases and their concepts that Jameson developed over those same years.

8. I spent a spatially disconcerted weekend in that hotel a decade at least before reading "Postmodernism." Reading Jameson not only brought back the immediacy of the experience as if it were yesterday, but also enabled me to understand it for the first time.

18 "Postmodernism, or The Cultural Logic of Late Capitalism," *New Left Review* 146 (January-February, 1984), 58–9. Further references to this work will be indicated in the text.

19 For Jameson, even something like anti-Semitism can be deciphered as utopian since it unifies people, even if through "a form of cultural envy which is at the same time a repressed recognition of the Utopian impulse" (*PU*, 288).

20 Here it might be worth questioning the ultimate use to Marxism of the utopian concept which Jameson adapts from Ernst Bloch and which is also evident in contemporary exhortations to keep a utopian vision alive on the embattled socialist left. Doesn't utopian vision finally entail a step outside history into a condescension by posterity in the form of ourselves? Why can't our awareness of the suffering required by capitalism be enough to sustain our confidence in Marxism to explain this suffering and the need to end it in a continuously participatory, if also regularly tragic, historical struggle?

21 The computer seems to me more appropriate than the reactor to exemplify both the postmodern sensorium and the postmodern community. But an example like the computer would undermine the logic by which Jameson reifies the category of "late capitalism" and incorporates it in a "diachronic sequence."

22 In this passage as elsewhere in "Postmodernism," Jameson acknowledges his debt to Ernest Mandel's *Late Capitalism*. But while Mandel is also a superstructuralist, and can even still refer to ideology as "false consciousness," the ideology produced by his late capitalism is far less invasive than that produced by Jameson's. Until its last two sentences, the following

passage from Mandel anticipates virtually the whole of Jameson's postmodernist argument. But then those two sentences open up a space that Jameson's argument won't allow:

> To the captive individual, whose entire life is subordinated to the laws of the market— not only . . . in the sphere of production, but also in the sphere of consumption, recreation, culture, art, education, and personal relations, it appears impossible to break out of the social prison. "Every-day experience" reinforces and internalizes the neo-fatalist ideology of the immutable nature of the late capitalist social order. All that is left is the dream of escape—through sex and drugs, which in their turn are promptly industrialized. The fate of the one-dimensional man seems to be wholly predetermined. *In reality, however, late capitalism is not a completely organized society at all. It is merely a hybrid and bastardized combination of organization and anarchy*. (Ernest Mandel, *Late Capitalism* [London: New Left Books, 1975], 503, 502; my emphasis)

For a critique of the technological determinism common to Mandel and Jameson and by now widely shared on the "post-Marxist" left, see Ellen Meiksins Wood, *The Retreat from Class: A New 'True' Socialism* (London: Verso, 1986), esp. Ch. 4, "The Autonomization of Ideology and Politics."

13 The title of Davis's chapter on Marxism is "Subject in a Marxism without Guarantees." For a critique of Jameson's teleology parallel to mine, but undertaken on behalf of Lyotard's postmodernism, see Haynes Horn, "Jameson's Strategies of Containment," in *Postmodernism, Jameson, Critique*, ed. Douglas Kellner (Washington, D.C.: Maisonneuve Press, 1989), 268–300.

14 "Jameson provides very vivid and suggestive examples to illustrate his theory, yet they are only examples and only illustrative. One gets little sense of an interest in counter-tendencies and the openness and contingency of the lived structure of history as it is produced and reproduced, albeit blindly, by individuals trapped together in competitive struggles and interdependencies in their everyday lives." (Mike Featherstone, "Postmodernism, Cultural Change, and Social Practice," *Postmodernism, Jameson, Critique*, 128)

CHAPTER 7

1 Adam Hochschild's *King Leopold's Ghost* (Boston: Houghton Mifflin, 1998), a history of the horrors imposed on the Congo in its initial colonization by capitalism, was published in the same year as *The Poisonwood Bible* and could be joined to it in a diptych.

2 Barbara Kingsolver, *The Poisonwood Bible* (New York: HarperFlamingo, 1998), 9. Further references to this work will be indicated in the text.

3 Walter A. Davis, *Inwardness and Existence* (Madison, Wis.: University of Wisconsin Press, 1989), 194.

INDEX

A

B

C

L

M

P

U

V

W

Z